THE **COMPLETE**
IDIOT'S
GUIDE TO

Knitting

by Becca Smith

ALPHA

A member of Penguin Group (USA) Inc.

ALPHA BOOKS

Published by the Penguin Group

Penguin Group (USA) Inc., 375 Hudson Street, New York, New York 10014, USA

Penguin Group (Canada), 90 Eglinton Avenue East, Suite 700, Toronto, Ontario M4P 2Y3, Canada (a division of Pearson Penguin Canada Inc.)

Penguin Books Ltd., 80 Strand, London WC2R 0RL, England

Penguin Ireland, 25 St. Stephen's Green, Dublin 2, Ireland (a division of Penguin Books Ltd.)

Penguin Group (Australia), 250 Camberwell Road, Camberwell, Victoria 3124, Australia (a division of Pearson Australia Group Pty. Ltd.)

Penguin Books India Pvt. Ltd., 11 Community Centre, Panchsheel Park, New Delhi—110 017, India

Penguin Group (NZ), 67 Apollo Drive, Rosedale, North Shore, Auckland 1311, New Zealand (a division of Pearson New Zealand Ltd.)

Penguin Books (South Africa) (Pty.) Ltd., 24 Sturdee Avenue, Rosebank, Johannesburg 2196, South Africa

Penguin Books Ltd., Registered Offices: 80 Strand, London WC2R 0RL, England

International Standard Book Number: 978-1-61564-051-5
Library of Congress Catalog Card Number: 2010903642

12 11 10   8 7 6 5 4 3 2 1

Interpretation of the printing code: The rightmost number of the first series of numbers is the year of the book's printing; the rightmost number of the second series of numbers is the number of the book's printing. For example, a printing code of 10-1 shows that the first printing occurred in 2010.

Printed in the United States of America

Note: This publication contains the opinions and ideas of its author. It is intended to provide helpful and informative material on the subject matter covered. It is sold with the understanding that the author and publisher are not engaged in rendering professional services in the book. If the reader requires personal assistance or advice, a competent professional should be consulted.

The author and publisher specifically disclaim any responsibility for any liability, loss, or risk, personal or otherwise, which is incurred as a consequence, directly or indirectly, of the use and application of any of the contents of this book.

Most Alpha books are available at special quantity discounts for bulk purchases for sales promotions, premiums, fund-raising, or educational use. Special books, or book excerpts, can also be created to fit specific needs.

For details, write: Special Markets, Alpha Books, 375 Hudson Street, New York, NY 10014.

Publisher: *Marie Butler-Knight*

Associate Publisher: *Mike Sanders*

Senior Managing Editor: *Billy Fields*

Executive Editor: *Randy Ladenheim-Gil*

Senior Acquisitions Editor: *Karyn Gerhard*

Senior Development Editor: *Christy Wagner*

Production Editor: *Kayla Dugger*

Copy Editor: *Amy Borrelli*

Cover Designer: *Kurt Owens*

Book Designers: *William Thomas, Rebecca Batchelor*

Indexer: *Brad Herriman*

Layout: *Ayanna Lacey*

Proofreader: *Laura Caddell*

Contents

Introduction

I delight in all things handmade. To me, there's an aura and something magical in objects and clothing someone took the time and attention to create by hand. It's why I love museums, where you can see what people made with their hands generations ago. When you look at or touch something handcrafted, you are connecting with the creative spirit of the person who made it. Somewhere in the process of making the object, there was struggle, improvisation, frustration, and spontaneous problem-solving. Something handmade represents hours of challenges, both intellectual and physical. Such pieces usually don't look perfect (only machines make perfect stitches row after row), but that's part of their charm.

A person took raw materials and transformed them into a unique object or garment, giving you insight into the artist. He or she made choices in materials, colors, patterns, and texture. The piece is an expression of a moment, or series of moments. I am impressed with excellent craftsmanship. Did the person care about the concept, the finished product, or both? A handmade piece is a treasure to be cherished and passed down to another generation.

And so it is with knitting. Contemporary masters Kaffe Fasset, Nicky Epstein, Berta Karapetyan, and so many others have inspired me. They continue to explore the craft in fantastic ways. I have also seen wonderful, jaw-dropping work by people walking on the street or attending fiber shows. I've been known to stop people to ask them about a scarf or sweater they're wearing. I always look forward to complimenting them, especially if we engage in a discussion about how they made their piece. I love talking about the choices they made and how they came to making them.

As you go through the lessons of this book, you, too, will be making choices. What yarn will you use for a project? What color? Texture? Size? Even when you're following a pattern line by line, you have to make decisions along the way. Do you like the way the pattern looks with the yarn you chose? What if you change the stitch pattern? Will the pattern be more prevalent? Are the colors overpowering? Take joy in your decisions, knowing that if you don't like something, you can always rip it out! You are in control here. It's all up to you.

As far back as I can remember, I loved working with my hands. I really *have* to do it. I know something made with my hands will be unique because I never make anything the same way twice, and that gives me great pleasure. May you experience the same pleasure working with your hands. Enjoy!

How to Use This Book

Each chapter in this book is a lesson exploring techniques. (You will be using practice yarn to try them out and when you're finished, you'll be able to incorporate all your swatches into another project, a mini sampler!) One chapter builds on another, so by the end, you should be able to read and understand just about any pattern you pick up. Along the way, I ask you to "Swatch It!" and knit 15 stitch patterns you can later assemble into a sampler. On other exercises, you'll try out different knitting methods and techniques before you apply them to real-life projects.

I've divided this book into six parts:

In **Part 1, The Basics: It's All About Loops,** you get to know the materials and tools you need to get started. You also learn how to begin knitting by creating a foundation row of loops along with the two basic stitches: knit and purl.

In **Part 2, Knits and Purls: The V's and the Bumps,** you gain confidence and experience as you learn 13 increasingly difficult stitch patterns. You knit up each pattern in a square swatch that, when you combine them later, form a sweet sampler. Many of these patterns are incorporated into projects throughout the book.

In **Part 3, Shaping, Knitting in the Round, and More,** your knitting takes on new shapes and colors. Increasing and decreasing stitches are important techniques for making garments, and you learn those here. You also learn knitting in the round, which is used for a variety of projects, from handbags to sweaters. Learning how to change yarns and colors is an important element in many patterns.

Everyone wants great-fitting garments, and in **Part 4, Intermediate Techniques,** you learn how as you explore basic shaping and assembly techniques, including for sweaters, socks, and rugs.

The techniques and projects in **Part 5, Advanced Techniques,** are not out of reach for a new knitter. If you've followed through most of the chapters up to this point, you should be able to pick up intarsia (knitting with color), entrelac (knitting in geometric shapes), and felting (intentionally wetting and shrinking your knitting!).

You only need a pair of needles and some yarn to get started knitting, but later on you might want to have a full range of needles and other tools—along with a better understanding of all the fibers available to you. **Part 6, Yarns and Tools,** introduces you to all these things.

In the back of the book, you'll find two appendixes: a glossary full of knitting-related terms and abbreviations and an appendix of further resources to help you feed your need for more things knitting.

Extra Bits

Throughout the book, you'll see nuggets of extra information, neatly packaged in sidebar boxes. Here's what to look for:

A STITCH IN TIME

These sidebars are full of interesting facts about knitting and knitters.

DEFINITION

Look to these sidebars for straightforward definitions of knitting terms, along with their abbreviations.

JAZZING IT UP

Check out these sidebars for creative ways to personalize your projects.

UNRAVELING

Like the unraveling of your stitches, this sidebar gives you advice on avoiding or correcting problems.

Acknowledgments

There's a great and possibly overused saying: "There is no *I* in *team*." The sentiment is so true, and the undertaking of this book was really a team endeavor. So many people around me helped in one way or another, and I sincerely thank them all.

I would not have written this book if it hadn't been for Steve Corcoran. Look Strategies marketing guru extraordinaire, he got wind of the opportunity and suggested my name. You don't say "no" to Steve. He is the eternal optimist and cheerleader, and he introduced me to my literary agent, Marilyn Allen. Marilyn and I clicked immediately, and she has provided tremendous guidance through the process, always positive and encouraging.

Some people are great knitters, but few have more imagination and enthusiasm than Susan Thompson. Susan helped with several of the pieces that needed designing and knitting.

Thanks to Janette Higgins, Jennie Dawes, and Jackie Smith, who took on additional responsibilities at the office to keep everything running smoothly. Janette and Jennie also proofed and reproofed chapter after chapter. They provided moral support and laughter along the way, as did my sister Shelley Ziech. No one can sell like Shelley, and she is a wonderful spirit at our shows.

Good friends always see you through the challenges in your life. My thanks to my wonderful friends Liz Tekus, owner of Fine Points—my local yarn shop (LYS); Kathy O'Neill, whose voice and presence is like a burst of sunshine; Penelope Taylor, editor of *Knit 'N Style* magazine and the person who guided me through my first book; Dora Tang, friend and knitter who literally lent her hands to this book; and last but never least, Suzanne Cohan-Lange, artist and best friend, and the person who knows the metaphors in my life.

My thanks to my friends and colleagues in the yarn business, including Bjorn Coodt of Coloratura Yarns, Jeannie Duncan of Fiesta Yarns, Barry Klein of Trendsetter Yarns, Warren Wheelock of Berroco Yarns, Angelo Fernandez of Aslan Trends, and Peggy Jo Wells of Brown Sheep. Many of the fabulous fibers featured in the patterns in this book were generously provided by their companies.

I sincerely thank Karyn Gerhard, Randy Ladenheim-Gil, and Christy Wagner, my editors. Their support, encouragement, and constructive comments helped me immensely.

Since I founded BagSmith, I have been so fortunate to have the involvement of my mother, Jean Ruben. She has been and continues to be a source of inspiration to me and all who know her. She shared her love of knitting and all things handmade with me as a child and taught me to be open to opportunities in life. If you ever see our BagSmith booth at a yarn show, look for Jean. She's the one sitting on a camping couch teaching someone to knit or crochet.

Photographer, actor, and my son, E. B. Smith, provided the photography throughout the book. We worked so well together, and it was my greatest joy to collaborate with him. My daughter-in-law, Moira Begale Smith, modeled the clothes so beautifully, as did granddaughter Kaelin Smith, Kasia Januszewski, and brand-new friend Finnegan Maisch. Having family members and friends participate is one of the great pleasures of a project like this.

My final thanks goes to my husband, Herb, the best swifter on the planet, partner, and friend, whose support for my activities never wavers.

Trademarks

The Basics: It's All About Loops

Knitting isn't a mystery. It's a process of working with needles and yarn to create loops. The loops are worked in rows and with each row your knitting grows. In Part 1, you learn about the yarn and tools you need to get started, how to work your loops on to and off your needles, and the two basic stitches—knit and purl.

Part 1 also includes instructions for casting on (putting loops on your needles), creating a foundation row, working them with the knit and purl stitches, and binding off (securely taking them off the needles with a finished edge). The steps in Part 1 are essential building blocks for the chapters in the rest of the book, so take your time and learn the basics.

You'll also have the opportunity to try two methods of knitting: Continental and English. Some knitters are more comfortable with one or the other. Try both and see which one suits you best.

Getting Started Knitting

In This Chapter

- Selecting your yarn
- Working with yarn—and avoiding tangles and knots!
- Choosing your needles

You don't need a lot of fancy tools and costly equipment to get started knitting. Along with this book, you only need two more things to get started: some yarn you like and a pair of needles. With these three items, you can enter the wonderful world of knitting.

And with a little practice and by working through the lessons in this book, you'll be able to pick up any pattern or knitting book and make a project, start to finish.

First Things First: The Yarn

I won't get into all the many types, sizes, and fibers of yarn here—that could almost be a whole book itself! But for now, let's focus on the yarn you'll need both for practice and for the projects in this book.

Where do you find yarn? Craft retailers and your local yarn shop (LYS) are your best sources. It's best not to order online at the beginning until you better understand weights, fiber content, and textures.

Choosing Your Yarn

Here are some tips for choosing the ideal practice yarn for the "Swatch It!" sections:

- *Weight:* Choose an inexpensive bulky weight. With the heavier yarn, you'll be better able to see and work with the stitches.
- *Color:* Make it a light color so you can easily see the stitches.

- *Texture:* The smoother the yarn, the better for learning the basic skills.

- *Fiber content:* Acrylics are great for beginners because they're inexpensive. Wool or wool blends are fine as well.

Yarn is available in several forms, including balls, skeins, and hanks.

The Yarn Council of America has developed a system for categorizing yarn according to weight. For example, chunky, bulky, or craft weight is represented by the number 5 on the label. Some imported yarns don't have the yarn weight number on the label. You can instead look for the needle size to be sure you have the right yarn.

Each project pattern tells you the suggested yarn, weight, texture, color, etc., so I won't go into all of that here. But I will say this: you should love the feel and the color of your project yarns. Part of the joy of this craft is falling in love with the fiber. Some of us knitters have earned our Yarnaholic, Fiber Floozy, and Yarn Junky nicknames! We collect yarn to use for future projects—or just because we love the feel and color. Our *stashes* can be enormous, like a kitchen cabinet full of ingredients for future concoctions. Like chocoholics flocking to a chocolatier, we fiberholics can't pass up a yarn shop and often travel out of our way to visit one. Yes, I admit to being in this group, although I refer to myself as a *stashionista!*

DEFINITION

A knitter's collection of yarn is known as his or her **stash.** This can include full skeins and balls or odds and ends left over from various projects. Some knitters, called swappers, trade yarn from their stash through online communities and knitting guilds.

You'll be working with your project yarn for a while, so be sure the yarn's characteristics please you. I've abandoned a few projects over the years because the fiber was impossible, difficult, or simply unpleasant in my hands.

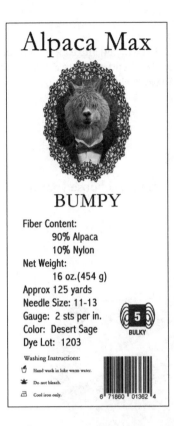

Alpaca Max

BUMPY

Fiber Content:
  90% Alpaca
  10% Nylon
Net Weight:
  16 oz.(454 g)
Approx 125 yards
Needle Size: 11-13
Gauge: 2 sts per in.
Color: Desert Sage
Dye Lot: 1203

5 BULKY

Washing Instructions:
  Hand wash in luke warm water.
  Do not bleach.
  Cool iron only.

6 71860 01362 4

Yarn labels vary by manufacturer, but most include weight, yardage, needle size, fiber content, and color.

You'll be making several projects over the next few chapters as you learn some basic skills, and you can change yarns each time if you like. Just be sure the yarn is about the same weight from project to project because we use the same needles throughout Part 1.

Some yarns come in balls while others come in *skeins* and still others come in *hanks*. Begin with a smooth yarn that has about 100 yards in the ball or skein.

Yarn suppliers often distribute hanks of yarn to better show the characteristics and color of the fiber.

Tools of the Trade: Needles

Now that you know what yarn you'd like to use, it's time to choose your needles.

Knitting needles are described and labeled in two ways: diameter and length. Most if not all yarn labels list the recommended needle size or range of needle sizes for that specific yarn. You can use this as a general guide, or find the needles that work best for you.

I suggest you begin with straight needles, preferably U.S. size 10.5 (6.5mm). The number refers to the diameter of the needle. It doesn't matter if they're wooden, bamboo, plastic, or metal needles. I find that yarn slides better on wooden or metal needles, and some people like beginning with the wood or plastic because the stitches don't fall off as easily.

Like yarn, choose needles you're comfortable with because you'll be using these needles for the first four parts of this book. Eventually, you will also need circular and double-pointed needles in the same size, but that's not until later.

A STITCH IN TIME

Julia Hopson of Penzance in Cornwall, England, holds the Guinness world record for knitting with the largest needles. They were 2½ inches in diameter and more than 31½ inches long!

The Least You Need to Know

- To begin knitting, you only need a few things: yarn, knitting needles, … and this book!
- When choosing your yarn, select one that looks good, feels good, and fits your project.
- Winding your yarn into a ball makes it easier to work with—and transport!
- The knitting needles you choose should feel good in your hands and work well with the yarn you've chosen.

Basic Stitch #1: Knit

In This Chapter

- Casting on—it's loopy!
- The knit stitch
- Binding off—closing the loops

I've said it before, but it bears repeating: there is no mystery to knitting. It is simply a process of working with needles to make various combinations of loops with yarn. That's it! Stitch patterns are combinations of loops in rows. Endless combinations of stitch patterns exist, and we explore many of them in this book.

There are two main stitches to learn: knit and purl. Once you've mastered these two stitches, you can knit almost anything using these stitches in different combinations. This chapter begins your adventure with the knit stitch.

Swatch It!

Why swatch? For many reasons, including checking your gauge (which I talk more about later). Making swatches is an easy way to try out new techniques and stitch patterns. You'll also see your technique improve as your cast-ons, stitches, and bind-offs become more even. The swatches are also useful references for stitch patterns.

Some knitters keep their swatches for future reference. As you go through the "Swatch It!" sections in this book, testing out your stitches, keep those swatches. You'll combine them into a fun project in a later chapter.

The Foundation Row: Casting On

Casting on is the first step in any knitting project. It is the process of putting loops on one of the needles. The cast-on stitches are called the *foundation row*.

JAZZING IT UP

A word about right and left handedness: knitting is a two-handed endeavor. Both hands are part of the entire process in all your projects. Because you're using both hands, it doesn't really matter which hand is doing what. Some left-handed knitters prefer to hold the working yarn in their left hand while knitting as a right-hander. If this isn't comfortable for you, you can reverse all the instructions. Remember to mentally reverse all the photos, too.

Here's how to do a simple cast-on:

1. Draw about 12 inches from the ball of yarn and make a loop at approximately the 12-inch mark.

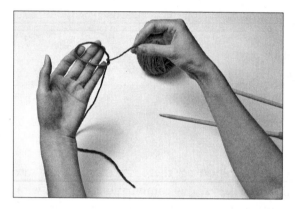

2. Wind the yarn around itself like the first step in tying your shoe. Using your right hand to hold one of the needles and your left hand to hold the loop, put one of the needles through the loop.

3. Holding the *tail* in one hand and the needle and *working yarn* in the other, gently tug the tail so the stitch is snug on the needle, but not too tight. The stitch should move easily along the needle.

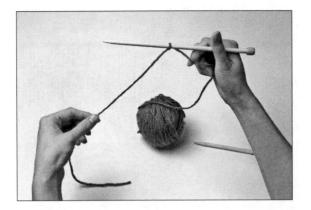

 DEFINITION

The yarn coming from the ball is the **working yarn,** while the 12-inch piece of yarn is the **tail.** The stitches created in the simple cast-on form the **foundation row.**

You have now cast on your first stitch! The journey of a thousand projects begins with just one stitch, as they say, but you need more. So let's cast on 18 more stitches. Here's how to add more loops to your needle:

1. Continue holding the needle in your right hand. Using your left hand, create a loop with the working yarn that crosses underneath the needle. (It doesn't matter, at this point, how you hold your yarn and needle. I explain the proper way to hold both coming up later in this chapter.)

2. Slip the loop onto the needle, with the working yarn coming through the loop and facing toward you.

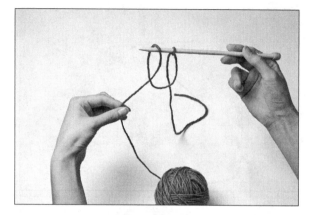

3. Pull the working yarn so the stitch is snug on the needle, but not too tight. Remember to keep the stitches loose so they're easy to work with later.

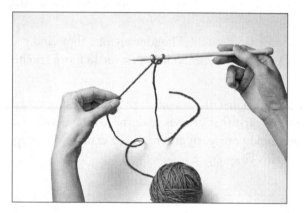

4. Once you get the hang of it, you can try this quicker technique to get the loops on the needle: pick up the working yarn with your thumb, and loop it around your thumb with a quick flip. Slide the needle under the working end, through the loop.

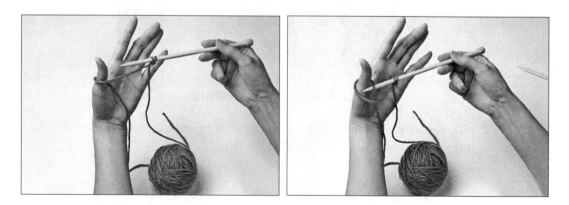

5. Repeat this process until you have 18 loops, or stitches, on your needle.

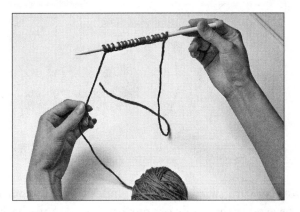

UNRAVELING

The first cast-on stitch is counted as part of all the stitches in the foundation row. While you're still learning, it's a good idea to count your stitches after each row. Drop a stitch? I cover how to fix that later.

Working the Knit Stitch

Now that you have your foundation row, you're ready to use those loops in your first knitted row! There are two techniques for holding the yarn and working the stitches:

- The *Continental* method, where you hold the working yarn with your left hand

- The *English* method, where you hold the working yarn with your right hand

The Continental method uses fewer movements, and many people feel it's the faster, more-efficient way to knit. Try both of them and see which one is more comfortable for you. Whichever way you choose, the stitches will all look the same.

Doing the Continental

The Continental method originated in Europe. Most professional knitters prefer this approach. It's the method I learned as a child from my grandmother and mother.

Here's how it's done:

1. Hold the needle with the stitches (the foundation row) in your left hand.

2. Wind the working yarn twice around the index finger of your left hand. The working yarn should be against the inside of your hand, not on the back of your hand. You'll use your index finger to help you position the yarn so you can easily pick it up with the right needle and maintain even tension.

3. Holding the empty needle in your right hand, insert the point into the first stitch on the left needle. The point should go into the first loop and from the left side of the stitch. Be sure you push the needle in far enough so you can wrap the yarn around the tip.

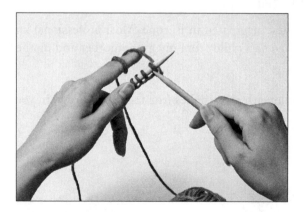

4. Using your left index finger, wind the yarn around the tip of the right (empty) needle from front to back.

5. With the right needle, pull the wrapped yarn through the loop toward you. You should now have 1 loop on your right needle.

6. Pull the right needle slightly to the right to slip the original stitch (loop) off the left needle. Be sure you don't pull the yarn too tight.

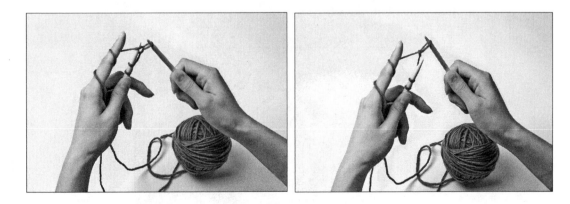

7. Repeat this process for the remaining 17 stitches. You've just completed your first row of knitting—congratulations!

Now, it's time to turn your work, or start the second row.

You always want to keep the needle with the stitches in your left hand and the needle with the working yarn in your right. So at the end of your first row, transfer the needle with the stitches to your left hand. This is called the ready position. Time to repeat row 1!

Continue knitting each row until you have a piece about 5 inches long. This combination of stitches and rows creates a stitch pattern called the *garter stitch*.

> **DEFINITION**
>
> The **garter stitch** is one of the most common stitch patterns, found in everything from scarves to sweaters. It's quite simple: knit every stitch in all rows. Look for it the next time you shop for a knitted piece.

When turning your work and changing needles from the right to the left, be sure you don't add an additional loop at the beginning of the row. Start with your yarn in back in the ready position to knit.

The English Method

Many people refer to the English method as one where you "throw" the yarn. There's really no throwing involved. The name refers to the use of the right hand in wrapping the working yarn around the left needle.

To throw or not to throw? I'll let you decide which method is right for you after trying this next swatch.

1. Begin by casting on 18 stitches.

2. Hold the needle with the foundation row stitches in your left hand with the working yarn on the right side. Hold the empty needle in your right hand with the yarn wrapped around your right index finger.

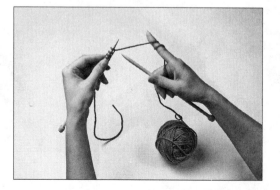

3. Insert the right needle into the first stitch from the front to the back and from the left side of the loop. This creates an X, with the right needle below the left. Hold the X between your left thumb and index finger.

4. With your right hand, wind the working yarn around the tip of the left needle from the left to the right, over the top of the needle.

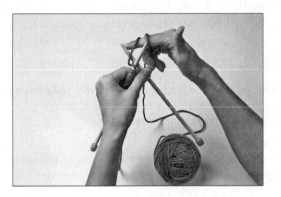

5. Using the right needle, pull the wrapped yarn through the loop to rest on the right needle.

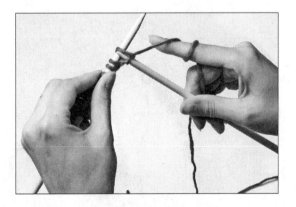

6. Slide off the rest of the original loop from the left needle, and continue with the other stitches in the row.

You've finished the first row! Now turn your work so the needle with the stitches is in your left hand and the working yarn is on the right side, and continue knitting until the piece measures 4⅞ inches.

Binding Off

Now that you have all the rows of your first swatch completed, you need to learn how to take the stitches off the needle without everything coming apart. This is called *binding off.*

 DEFINITION

When you **bind off,** you take the stitches off your needle while closing the loops to form a finished edge. As you learn this technique, be careful not to pull your bind-off stitches too tight. A tight bind-off results in a curled edge.

The bind-off is like a series of loop closures with a knot at the end. Although it may seem a little awkward, binding off is quite simple. Here are the steps:

1. Knit 2 stitches. Mentally label the first stitch on the right needle "stitch A" and the second stitch "stitch B."

2. Insert the point of the left needle into stitch A.

3. Lift stitch A over stitch B.

4. Continue pulling A over the point of the right needle.

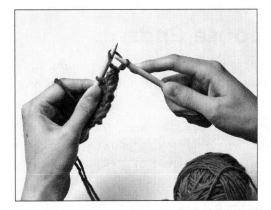

5. Now you should have 1 stitch on the right needle. Knit the remaining stitch on the left needle so you have 2 stitches on the right.

6. Repeat steps 2 through 4.

7. When you get to the last stitch, cut the yarn and pull the end through the last loop.

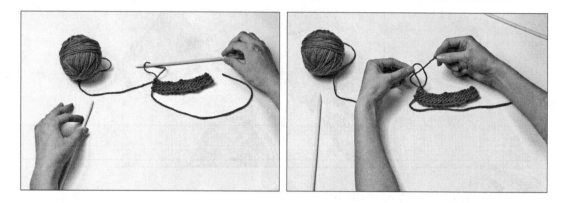

When you first learn to bind off, be careful that you don't pull the working yarn too tight. This will cause the top edge to curve, as in the right swatch in the following photo. If you do manage a tight bind-off, don't worry. You can address this later in one of several ways. In your next swatch, just practice with a relaxed approach to your bind-off.

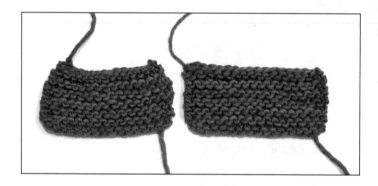

Notice the two bind-off edges. One is straight, and the other is curved where the stitches were bound off tightly.

Wrapping Up Loose Ends

After binding off, you'll have two tails, one at the beginning and one at the end. You can hide these tails in your knitting by weaving them into the stitches on the wrong side of your work. Here's how:

1. Using a large-eye darning needle, thread the yarn through 6 or 7 stitches along the bottom row of the wrong side (WS), following the direction of the knitting. If you're working on a scarf or other piece that does not have a wrong side, do your best to conceal the ends along the bottom or side of the piece.

2. Cut the yarn near the last woven stitch.

Alternatively, you can also use the tails to sew pieces together.

A STITCH IN TIME

As a new knitter, you are in good company. According to the Craft Yarn Council of America, approximately 54 million women can knit or crochet. This represents a 51 percent increase over the last 10 years. Another way to look at it: 36 percent of American women know how to knit or crochet—and this doesn't even include the growing number of men involved with the craft!

Project: Garter Stitch Skinny Scarf

Believe it or not, you now have all the basic skills you need to make a scarf, so go for it! This project is very easy and reinforces the three techniques you learned in this chapter: cast on, knit stitch, and bind off.

You can adapt this simple scarf to many sizes. The pattern calls for 14 stitches, but you can easily widen it to 18 or 20 for a teenager or adult.

The scarf is made with the garter stitch, which basically means you knit every row. This stitch is used in many patterns for shawls, sweaters, hats, and many other projects. Some patterns combine it with other stitches or combinations of stitches.

Finished size:

> The finished size varies according to the yarn you use and your gauge. You can decide how short or long to make it. A good scarf length for an adult is about 40 to 50 inches.

Materials:

> 130 yards worsted or chunky weight yarn
>
> U.S. 10.5 (6.5mm) straight needles
>
> Large-eye darning needle
>
> Scissors
>
> Measuring tape

Gauge:

> Not critical

Abbreviations:

BO	bind off
CO	cast on
k	knit
st(s)	stitch(es)

A STITCH IN TIME

Abbreviations in knitting are usually pretty obvious. Sometimes they're just the first letter of a word, like the one for knit (k); other times they are two or three letters, like the abbreviation for stitches (sts). Until you get used to seeing the abbreviations only, I'll still use the full name with the abbreviations in parentheses.

Cast on (CO) 14 stitches (sts).

Row 1: Knit (k) all stitches (sts).

Row 2: Knit (k) and continue (cont) knitting all rows until the piece measures 60 inches.

Bind off (BO) and cut the yarn, leaving an 8-inch tail.

For some fun, you could make three Skinny Scarves in three complementary colors and sew them together lengthwise to create a wide scarf or even a shawl. You could also add small pins or appliqués at each end, embroider a design, or sew on some interesting fiber the length of the scarf.

The Least You Need to Know

- The two main stitches in knitting are the knit stitch and the purl stitch.
- Casting on is the method you use to create the stitches of the foundation row.
- You can learn to knit using the Continental method or the English method.
- Binding off is the process for completing a knitted edge, taking the stitches off the needle and closing the loops as you go.

Basic Stitch #2: Purl

In This Chapter

- Making a long-tail cast-on
- The purl stitch
- Combining knits and purls
- Following your first pattern

Now that you've conquered the knit stitch in Chapter 2, it's time to learn the other most important stitch of the craft: the purl stitch.

The purl stitch is nothing more than a backward knit stitch. When you knit, you carry the yarn in the *back* of the left needle. When you purl, you carry the yarn in *front* of the left needle. The front of a knit stitch appears like a V shape, and the back of the stitch appears as a bump—that bump is the shape of a purl stitch.

New knitters often dislike purling because it seems awkward. It's like learning to swim and loving the crawl while hating the backstroke. Be patient. The more comfortable you become with the backstroke, the more you relax with it. The same goes for the purl stitch.

The Long-Tail Cast-On

Before beginning the purl stitch, let's learn another cast-on method called the long-tail cast-on. This method is a commonly used one, and it's called for in some of the projects in this book. It reminds me of a school yard game I played with friends in grammar school called "cat's cradle" because of the way you wrap the yarn around your fingers. The long-tail cast-on gives you a smooth, even edge, which is desirable for many patterns.

Like the simple cast-on you learned in Chapter 2, you begin by holding the needle in your right hand:

1. Make a loop like the one you used for the simple cast-on, leaving a 16-inch tail.

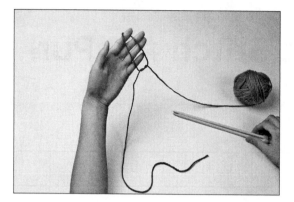

2. Place the loop on the needle with the tail hanging near you and the working yarn away from you.

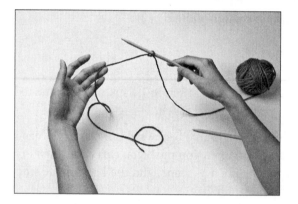

3. Using your left thumb and index finger, form a V shape with the working yarn and the tail, and hold it out from the needle like a sling shot.

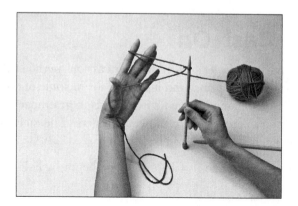

4. With your left pinkie and ring fingers, hold the 2 strands of yarn under the needle and against your palm.

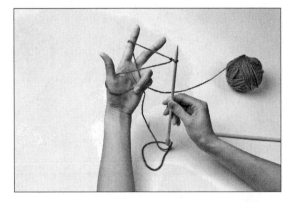

5. Insert the needle under the yarn to the left of your thumb, and bring it up through the loop around your thumb.

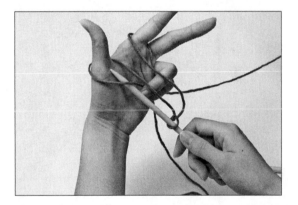

6. Angle the needle around to pick up the yarn nearest your index finger.

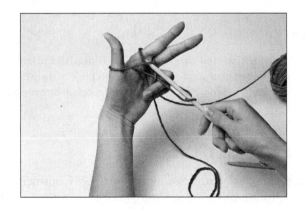

7. Pull the yarn back through the thumb loop where you started.

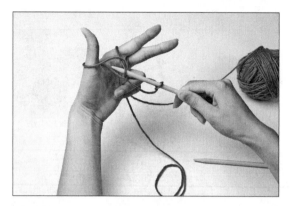

8. Let the thumb loop fall off, just like an old stitch from the left needle. Your new stitch is now on the right needle.

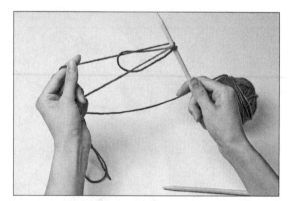

How long should your tail be for long-tail cast-on? It can vary according to the size of the needle and the thickness of the yarn. For the size 10.5 needles you're using now, figure about 1 inch per stitch for the tail, and remember that you need some left over for winding in at the end!

UNRAVELING

If your cast-on is too tight, your stitches will probably be too hard to knit off. For the next cast-on, remember to keep your stitches looser. For this project, try using a larger needle for the foundation row and then knit off this row using the regular-size needle.

Working the Purl Stitch

Just like the knit stitch, there are two methods for purling: Continental or English. Choose whichever method you preferred from your knitting lesson in Chapter 2, and let's go!

Doing the (Reverse) Continental

You'll be making a swatch just as you did with the knit stitch. Use your practice yarn and size 10.5 needles. Don't worry about how your stitches look at first. The more you practice, the more even the stitches will be.

1. Cast on 18 stitches using the long-tail cast-on.

2. Hold the needle with the stitches in your left hand, with the working yarn hanging on the right.

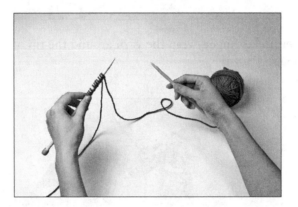

3. Bring the working yarn toward you, in front of the needle, and wrap the yarn around your left index finger. Your index finger should help guide the yarn around the point of the right needle.

4. With the other needle in your right hand, insert the point through the front of the first stitch.

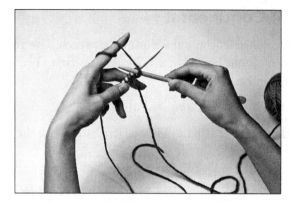

5. Using your left index finger, wrap the yarn around the tip of the right needle counterclockwise.

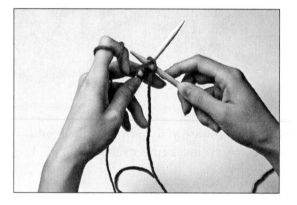

6. Angle the wrapped yarn downward, and pull it through the original stitch.

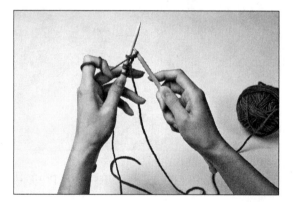

7. Let the old stitch drop off the left needle. The new stitch will be on the right needle.

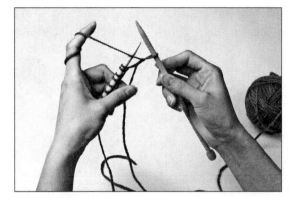

8. Repeat for the remaining stitches.

Take a look at the stitch on your right needle. See the bump just under the needle? This is how the purl stitch looks.

The English Method

If you're more comfortable "throwing the yarn," here are the instructions for the English method:

1. Cast on 18 stitches using the long-tail cast-on.

2. Hold the needle with the cast-on row and the working yarn in your left hand, with the working yarn on the right side, hanging downward. The empty needle should be in your right hand.

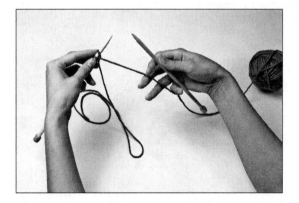

3. Insert the right needle into the first stitch, to the right side of the stitch, with the right point toward you, forming an X.

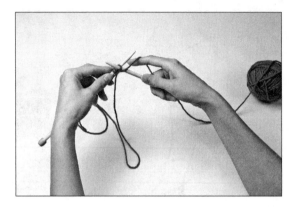

4. Use your left thumb to hold the crossed needles in place.

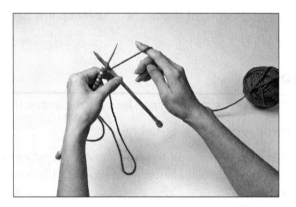

5. With your right hand, wrap the working yarn around the point of the right needle counterclockwise.

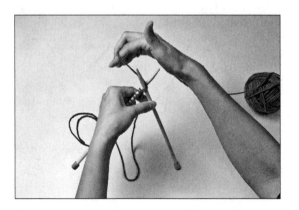

6. Bring the wrapped loop through the original stitch toward the back.

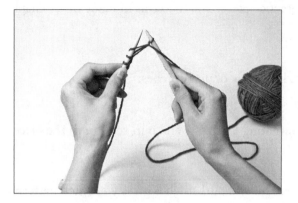

7. The new loop of yarn (stitch) should be on your right needle.

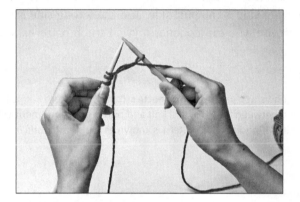

8. Repeat for remaining stitches on left needle.

A STITCH IN TIME

Now that you've conquered the cast-on, knit stitch, purl stitch, and bind-off, you can join the ranks of knitters who display their talents on World Wide Knit in Public (WWKIP) Day. The event began in 2005 as a way for knitters to come together and enjoy each other's company. It's now the largest knitter-run event in the world, all coordinated by volunteers. In 2005, 25 local events were held around the world. The event has grown with each subsequent year, and now hundreds of events take place in many countries. WWKIP Day is scheduled annually for the third Saturday and Sunday of June.

Combining Knits and Purls

It's time to make a practice piece. You'll do this in many other chapters, so get used to swatching:

Swatch It!

1. Continue with the row of purl stitches.

2. For the next row, use the knit stitch.

3. Continue alternating knit rows and purl rows until the piece measures 4⅞ inches and bind off.

Switching off between knit and purl stitches gives you stitch patterns. You've just completed a swatch using the *stockinette stitch* pattern, knit 1 row and purl 1 row. One side will look very flat and the other very bumpy. In the stockinette stitch, the knit side is the "right side" (RS), and the purl or bumpy side is the "wrong side" (WS). In the reverse stockinette stitch pattern, the opposite applies: the right side is the purl side, and the wrong side is the knit side. With knit and purl in your repertoire, you can conquer myriad stitch patterns.

DEFINITION

Here's your second stitch pattern: **stockinette stitch.** The pattern is knit 1 row and purl 1 row. Alternating between these rows of knit and purl produces a smooth side and a bumpy side. In the United Kingdom, this pattern is known as the *stocking stitch.*

A Little Help

New knitters are sometimes confused about where they are in a pattern sequence. Here are some tips that might help:

• Finish the row before putting down your knitting. This prevents stitches from falling off in the middle of the row.

• Count your stitches, and count your rows. Keep track on a piece of paper as you work, or you could use a stitch counter.

• As you finish each row, compare the right side (RS) and wrong side (WS) so you can visually recognize both patterns.

Project: Two-Stitch Hat

Now it's time to apply what you learned in this chapter by making a two-stitch hat.

You can easily adjust the size of this simple hat for children and adults.

This simple hat can be made for a child or adult. All you have to do is knit a rectangle, sew up one seam, and create a drawstring top with one of the tails.

Finished size:

> *Child:* 8 inches W×10 inches H
>
> *Adult S/M:* 9 inches W×11 inches H
>
> *Adult L/XL:* 10 inches W×12 inches H

Materials:

> Approximately 160 yards worsted weight yarn
>
> U.S. 10.5 (6.5mm) straight needles
>
> 4×6-inch piece of cardboard
>
> Large-eye darning needle
>
> Scissors
>
> Measuring tape

Gauge:

4 sts = 1 inch; 5 rows = 1 inch (This is approximate and may vary according to your yarn and the size of your stitches.)

When you look at project patterns, they will often begin with a stitch guide where the stitch patterns are explained. Here's an example:

Stitch pattern:

There are two stitch patterns in this project: garter stitch and stockinette. The project pattern begins with the garter because it is stretchy and is the part of the hat that goes over the head first.

Garter stitch: *K all sts and all rows.

Stockinette: *K 1 row, p 1 row; rep until piece measures correct length.

Note the use of an asterisk (*). This indicates the beginning of the pattern.

Abbreviations:

*	indicates the beginning of a pattern
cont	continue
rep	repeat
RS	right side
WS	wrong side

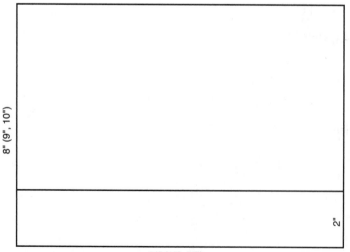

16" (18", 20")

Many patterns have schematics and charts to help you understand the shapes and dimensions of projects. Here you get the width and length of the flat, knitted piece that will be formed into the hat. The numbers in parenthesis indicate the dimensions for larger sizes.

Cast on (CO) 56 (64, 72) stitches (sts), leaving a 16-inch tail.

Row 1: Knit (k) all stitches (sts), and continue knitting all rows until the piece measures 2 inches (garter stitch).

Change to stockinette stitch—knit (k) 1 row, purl (p) 1 row—and continue (cont) until the piece measures 7 (8, 9) inches from the cast-on (CO) row.

Bind off (BO) and cut the yarn, leaving a 12-inch tail.

Change to stockinette stitch. Knit (K) 1 row, purl (p) 1 row.

Continue (cont) with stockinette stitch until the piece measures 11 (12, 13) inches from the foundation row to the top.

Bind off (BO), leaving a 12-inch tail.

UNRAVELING

Be careful with the 16-inch tail at the cast-on. It's very easy to begin knitting with this tail instead of the working yarn. If you do, you won't get very far and you'll have to go back!

When you get to this point, your knitting is finished and you're ready for assembly.

Finishing:

With a little sewing and the creation of a pompom for the top, your hat will soon be ready to wear:

1. Fold the piece in half with the wrong side (WS) or purl side on the outside and with the side edges meeting in the middle.

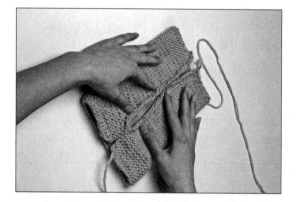

2. If the tail at the stockinette end is long enough, thread it through the needle and begin stitching up the edge at the first stitch of the garter stitch edge. If the tail isn't long enough, attach a long piece of yarn near the corner of one side and begin stitching up the edge.

3. Bring the needle back to the next stitch, and repeat. This is the *whipstitch*. After completing the seam, weave in all ends. You should now have a tube shape that's open on both ends.

DEFINITION

Many projects are finished using a common seaming technique called the **whipstitch,** named for the hand motion similar to whipping potatoes. It's an overhand stitch that will be seen from the outside and the inside.

4. With the other tail, you're going to create a drawstring closure. With your tube inside out (the finished side or knit side is facing inward), weave the yarn in and out of the top edge, which is the stockinette edge.

5. Once you've threaded the yarn all the way around the top edge, pull the end of the drawstring tightly to close the end of the tube. This will be the top of the hat. Pull it very tight so you don't leave a hole at the top. If there is a hole, you can sew it up.

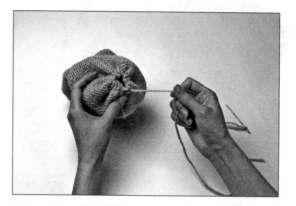

6. Weave the end through a few stitches, and knot it close to the last stitch.

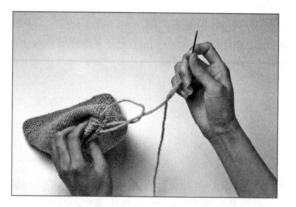

7. Sew up the hole, weave the tail into a few stitches, and cut the yarn.

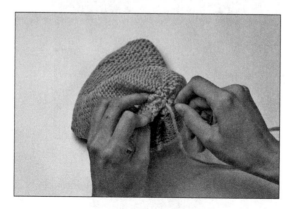

Pompom:

Now for the real topper!

1. Using the cardboard, wind the yarn around the 4-inch side of the board about 40 times.

2. Cut the end of the yarn, attach the darning needle to the tail, and slip the needle under one end of the wound yarn near the edge of the cardboard.

3. Securely tie a knot around the yarn at the end. To ensure tightness, knot it a second time.

4. Cut the yarn at the opposite end of the cardboard as evenly and cleanly as possible.

5. Wind a 10-inch length of yarn around the pompom about ½ inch from the top, and tie a knot. For added security, wind it around a second time and knot it.

6. Trim the ends so they are even.

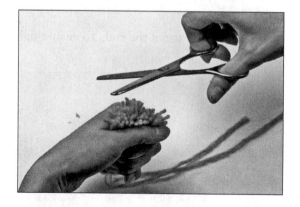

7. Sew the pompom to the top of the hat, and push the needle and yarn through to the inside.

8. Turn the hat inside out.

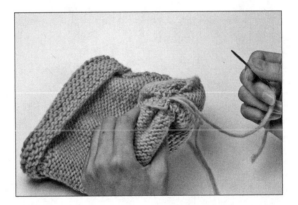

9. Secure the pompom from the inside by sewing it to the top of the hat.

10. Knot the end inside, and weave the end through some stitches. Turn the hat right side out and proudly place it on your head!

Congratulations! You've knitted your first hat!

The Least You Need to Know

- The purl stitch is the back side of the knit stitch. You can recognize it by the bump in front of the stitch.
- Combining knits and purls creates stitch patterns.
- You can purl using the Continental or English method. The results are exactly the same.
- The whipstitch is an overhand stitch used to close seams.

Knits and Purls: The V's and the Bumps

Stitch patterns are combinations of stitches and rows. Part 2 explores a variety of common stitches and teaches you how to knit them—and keep your bearings while doing so. By swatching each new stitch pattern, you gather the pieces you need for a sampler.

The patterns in Part 2 are divided into three groups. You begin with easy ones that are simple combinations of knits and purls. Then you move on to intermediate stitch patterns that include some additional techniques for combining stitches. The third group includes stitch patterns that have sequences over many rows. Move through these sequentially, and by the time you finish, you should be proficient enough to understand them. Tips for recognizing the right sides and wrong sides of knitted patterns are also included in this part.

Many of the patterns in Part 2 are used in projects you'll find in later chapters. The swatches you make of each pattern serve as a reference for your later work, and as you recognize the patterns you'll be able to say, "I can do that!"

What Makes a Stitch Pattern?

In This Chapter

- Combining stitches and rows to make stitch patterns
- Learning your right side from your wrong side
- Reading stitch patterns
- Gauge rules!

Stitch patterns are knitted rhythms and melodies. I often have songs and rhythms playing in my head while knitting patterns. Some are marches with strong one-two steps, like Sousa's "Stars and Stripes Forever." Others are like waltzes that glide over 3 stitches. Stitch patterns can be irregular like the 5/4 rhythms in Dave Brubeck's "Take Five" jazz composition. Young knitters might use jump rope rhymes or pop or rap lyrics for these patterns.

In books and online you can find hundreds of stitch patterns. You might invent some yourself, perhaps through a dropped stitch or other "mistake." I'm sure some patterns weren't intentional designs but instead became an interesting pattern through misunderstood instructions or interpretations. Some stitch patterns go forward and then back, reworking stitches after they're knitted the first time. More complex patterns extend over several rows and then repeat, almost like overlapping voices in a round (think "Three Blind Mice"). And some patterns are so complex that having any music or rhythms in your head will be a detriment to finishing the piece!

In the next four chapters, you learn stitches that demonstrate all these examples.

Right Sides and Wrong Sides

Some patterns are the same on both sides, like the garter stitch from Chapter 2. Other stitch patterns have two different sides, like the stockinette stitch in Chapter 3. If the sides aren't the same, the piece is said to have a right side (RS) and a wrong side (WS). When making a sweater, the right side would be the public side, or the side you see. The wrong side would be the stitches on the inside of the sweater against your skin.

Sometimes you might knit a pattern and decide the wrong side is the side you want seen. Just make the switch—it's your call.

Reading a Stitch Pattern

Once you're familiar with knitting abbreviations and symbols, stitch patterns are quite easy to read. They tell you the number of stitches in the pattern and the number of rows before it all repeats.

Here are two examples of stitch patterns, one simple and the other more complex:

Seed stitch:

(multiples of 2 sts plus 1)

Row 1: (RS) K1, *p1, k1; rep from * to end.

Rep Row 1.

Let's take a good look at this pattern. Below the title, "Seed Stitch," you have the number of stitches in the repeat—2 stitches plus 1 additional stitch. Pick up your needles and some practice yarn, and cast on multiples of 2 plus 1 additional stitch (6 sts plus 1 more, or 8 sts plus 1 more). That extra stitch is key to making the pattern work correctly.

Try the pattern. Knit 1 stitch, purl 1 stitch, knit 1 stitch, and continue to the end of the row. Turn your work and begin the second row. Your second row and all subsequent rows begin with a knit stitch just like the first row. The extra stitch allows for this and makes the pattern easy to remember.

You'll also notice after your first row you knit the purl stitches (when you see a bump) and purl the knit stitches (when you see a V). This makes it easy for you to find your place! It's a very basic pattern—a two-step or a slow march.

Now for a more complex pattern with a combination of stitches and rows:

Diamond brocade:

(multiples of 8 sts plus 1)

Row 1: (RS) K4, *p1, k7; rep from * to last 5 sts, p1, k4.

Row 2: P3, *k1, p1, k1, p5; rep from * to last 6 sts, k1, p1, k1, p3.

Row 3: K2, *p1, k3; rep from * to last 3 sts, p1, k2.

Row 4: P1, *k1, p5, k1, p1; rep from * to end.

Row 5: *P1, k7; rep from * to last st, p1.

Row 6: as per Row 4.

Row 7: as per Row 3.

Row 8: as per Row 2.

Let's try this pattern. Pick up your needles and your practice yarn, and cast on 18 stitches. Here are a few things to watch for as you work:

- This is an 8-row sequence. Check off each row as you go.

- Rows 6, 7, and 8 are repeats of Rows 4, 3, and 2, respectively.

- Knit all 8 rows to see the whole pattern.

- As you look at the right side (RS), you will see that the purl stitches form the diamond shapes in the pattern.

Because of the complexity of this pattern, I would keep the music turned way down.

Different Patterns, Varying Results

Some patterns pull together the stitches tightly, while other patterns are more elastic. Using the same number of stitches with the same yarn but different patterns can produce pieces of varying sizes.

This example shows the garter stitch next to the 2×2 rib stitch. Both swatches have the same number of stitches, but the dimensions are different.

Each one of these swatches has 12 stitches. The left one is a garter stitch. The right one is a 2×2 rib stitch (*k2, p2; rep from * to end). Alternating the knit and purl stitches in the rib stitch causes the stitches to pull closely together.

The All-Important Gauge

In knitting, *gauge* is the number of stitches and rows per inch. Calculating your gauge is a very important component of knitting. Every person knits a little differently. One may knit loosely while the next pulls the yarn tight. This doesn't matter much if you're just making scarves, but when you begin to work on garments, gauge becomes very important. You may need more or less stitches per inch, depending on how tightly or loosely you knit.

DEFINITION

Gauge is the number of stitches per inch and rows per inch of knitting.

Gauge depends on four things:

- Thickness of the yarn
- Size of the needle
- Your own style of knitting
- Stitch pattern

Look back at the previous photo with the two swatches. Each swatch was knitted on size 10.5 needles, with the same yarn, and with 24 stitches and 20 rows. That said, the shapes are very different. One is wider and taller, thanks to the stitch pattern.

Knitting a gauge swatch before beginning a project is a habit all knitters need to get into. Here are some guidelines for making swatches for a project:

- Always use your project yarn and the suggested needle size specified in the project pattern.

- Measure your gauge in the center of your swatch. You'll get a more reliable measure there than at the ends or sides.

- If your gauge doesn't match the gauge in the pattern, change needle sizes until you get the correct gauge. If you have too many stitches per inch, go up to a larger needle. If you have too few stitches per inch, go down a needle size.

Here are some guidelines to follow when measuring gauge:

The garter stitch gauge is 4 sts = 1 inch.

The rib stitch gauge is 5 sts = 1 inch.

Line up the ruler horizontally, even with the rows, to measure the number of stitches per inch.

Line up the ruler vertically, perpendicular to the rows, to measure the number of rows per inch.

You may think all this gauge swatching and measuring is tedious, but knitting projects are like puzzles, and to be sure the pieces fit together *and* fit the end user, the pieces must be the right size. If you're knitting a sweater for a friend, you want to avoid making it too big or too small. It needs to be just right!

> **UNRAVELING**
>
> When you first begin to knit and really get the hang of it, you may be tempted to just continue on without resting. This is when you'll probably make mistakes. Take a break and come back to it. Just remember this great Irish proverb: "If the knitter is weary, the baby will have no new bonnet."

Counting Stitches and Rows

Counting is *essential* as you learn new stitch patterns and work them into projects. You need to count stitches and count rows until you recognize where you are visually. Even when you're comfortable with a pattern, it's a good idea to keep track of your stitches. The method for counting the stitches is obvious—just go by the number of stitches on your needle. Counting rows is determined by the stitch pattern you're using.

Take a look at these three examples:

- In the garter stitch, every row of bumps (purl rows) is the equivalent of 2 rows.

- In the stockinette stitch, you count every V on the right side of the pattern.

- In the seed stitch, you count alternating bumps (purl stitches) for each row.

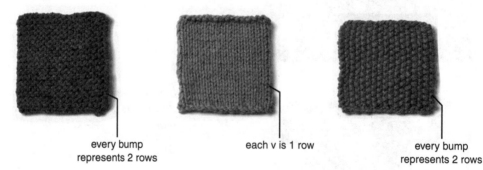

every bump
represents 2 rows

each v is 1 row

every bump
represents 2 rows

Here are three different stitch patterns and the key to counting the rows in each pattern.

You'll be able to count rows by finding the repeats in some patterns. More complex patterns are sometimes easier to look at because of the number of rows in the repeat, which can be more than 30! In these cases, be sure you keep track of your rows on a piece of paper or with a stitch counter.

Regular counting can help you avoid mistakes. But mistakes can be very important and lead you to new ideas and patterns. George Bernard Shaw once said, "A life spent making mistakes is not only more honorable, but more useful than a life spent doing nothing."

The Least You Need to Know

- Stitch patterns may be reversible and look the same on both sides, but others will be different on each side, creating a "right side" and a "wrong side."
- Your knitting gauge is very important, especially when you're making garments or pieces that must fit together. Gauge can vary according to yarn and needle size, and especially knitter to knitter.
- Counting your stitches and rows as you go helps you avoid mistakes.
- Taking the time to knit swatches enables you to check your gauge, see how your yarn works up, and practice the stitch pattern.

Easy Stitches

In This Chapter

- Mastering the seed stitch
- Working the moss stitch
- Putting in purl ridges
- Making the rib stitch

This group of 4 stitches contain simple combinations of knits and purls. Two-steps and four-beat marches come into my head with these stitches. These are easy stitch patterns to learn, and you will keep track of where you are without much problem. The seed stitch, moss stitch, and 2×2 rib are reversible, while the purl ridges have a right side and a wrong side. Swatching these stitches gives you great practice with the knit and purl stitches and shows you what happens when you combine them.

The Seed Stitch

Alternating between knit and purl stitches gives the seed stitch pattern a seedlike appearance.

Because you use an uneven number of stitches, every row begins with a knit stitch. If you have to use an even number for gauge purposes, the rows alternate beginning with a knit stitch and then a purl stitch.

The trick to the seed stitch is remembering to knit into the purl stitches, and purl into the knit stitches. This is a reversible pattern (like the garter stitch) and looks the same on both sides. It is a perfect stitch for reversible projects like scarves and shawls.

George Bernard Shaw once said America and England were two countries separated by a common language. Well, here is a knitting example. In the United Kingdom, this seed stitch is known as the moss stitch. In America, the moss stitch is a 4-row pattern we explore next.

Swatch It!

(multiples of 2 sts plus 1)

CO 17 sts.

Row 1: *K1, p1; rep from * to end.

Row 2: *P1, k1; rep from * to end.

Rep until piece measures 4⅞ inches, and BO.

The seed stitch looks exactly the same on both sides, and the purl stitches create a contrasting pattern to the knit stitches.

The Moss Stitch

The moss stitch is a 4-row pattern knitted in multiples of 4 stitches.

As you knit this pattern, you'll see "steps" emerging.

When you see a pattern noting the moss stitch, be sure it's not referring to the American seed stitch mentioned earlier. The moss stitch is sometimes called the double seed stitch, and like the seed stitch, it is a reversible pattern.

Swatch It!

(multiples of 4 sts)

CO 16 sts.

Row 1: (RS) *K2, p2; rep from * to end.

Rows 2 and 3: *P2, k2; rep from * to end.

Row 4: *K2, p2; rep from * to end.

Rep all 4 rows until piece measures 4⅞ inches.

BO in stitch pattern (st patt), *knitwise* and *purlwise*.

> **DEFINITION**
>
> **Knitwise** and **purlwise** are terms you'll see quite frequently in patterns. They simply mean that you're doing a procedure with a knit stitch or a purl stitch. In the moss stitch, you're asked to bind off in the stitch pattern. This means you knit the knit stitches as you bind them off and purl the purl stitches.

The Purl Ridge

This lovely 4-row pattern adds textural interest through the alternating knits and purls in the third row.

This is the right side of the purl ridge swatch (left) and the wrong side (right).

The front and back are different in this stitch pattern.

Swatch It!

(worked over an odd number of sts)

CO 17 sts.

Row 1: (RS) K.

Rows 2 and 4: P.

Row 3: K1, *p1, k1; rep from * to end.

Cont until piece measures 4⅞ inches.

BO.

The 2×2 Rib

This 2-row pattern is commonly used for cuffs, hems, collars, and edges because it makes a very stretchy fabric.

This is the right side of the 2×2 rib swatch (left) and the wrong side (right).

Notice that this pattern requires more stitches to make the 5×5-inch square because of the elasticity.

In this example, the front and back look exactly the same because an even number of knits and purls are used. Ribs can be any number of stitch combinations, but you will always knit the knit stitches and purl the purl stitches to form the vertical pattern of a basic rib.

Swatch It!

(even number of sts)

CO 26 sts.

Row 1: *K2, p2; rep to end.

Row 2: *P2, k2; rep to end.

Rep both rows until piece measures 4⅞ inches.

BO in st patt.

The Least You Need to Know

- Combinations of knit and purl stitches can create textural interest.
- Because of their elasticity, rib patterns are commonly used for cuffs, collars, and the bottom edges of sweaters.
- Knitwise and purlwise indicate how to do a procedure. For instance, if you're binding off purlwise, your yarn should be in front and all the bind-off stitches should be purls.

Intermediate Stitches

In This Chapter

- The mock rib stitch—smoother than regular ribs
- The basket weave—hardly a basket case!
- Meet the slip stitch
- The broken rib (better than it sounds!)

The stitches explored in this chapter involve more rows and additional ways of combining knits and purls. One stitch pattern involves a new technique called a slip stitch. You may recognize some of them from sweaters or textiles you have at home, especially the basket weave stitch. Go ahead and try them all.

The Mock Rib

Mock rib is a 2-row pattern worked over an odd number of stitches.

Several different versions of this stitch are available in books and online. Some include modified cables, while others feature slipped stitches. This chapter's pattern is a simple version, interesting from both the front and back. Notice the vertical and horizontal characteristics.

Swatch It!

(worked over uneven number of sts)

CO 17 sts.

Row 1: (RS) *K1, p1, k1; rep from * to end.

Row 2: P.

Rep Rows 1 and 2 until piece measures 4⅞ inches.

BO in st patt.

The right side (left) features strong vertical lines, and the purl stitches are dominant on the wrong side (right).

The Basket Weave

Basket weave stitches come in many variations, but they all look like woven patterns, hence the name.

This stitch is reversible. Each square has the same number of stitches whether or not you knit or purl.

Some versions of basket weave, like this one, are reversible, while others are different on the front and back.

This pattern is worked over 12 rows and multiples of 8 stitches. To create a 5×5-inch block, you'll add 1 *selvedge* knit stitch at the beginning and end of each row.

DEFINITION

A **selvedge** (sometimes spelled *selvage*) edge is created by adding a stitch or two at the beginning and end of each row of a stitch pattern. This gives the piece a firm edge and makes it easier to sew it to other pieces. In some stitch patterns, it can also eliminate curling at the edge. If you add a knit stitch at the beginning and end of each row, it can help you with counting the rows. Just look for the pattern it provides. You'll see a purl stitch every other row when you look at the right side.

Swatch It!

(multiples of 8 sts plus 2)

CO 18 sts.

K 2 rows and beg st patt.

Row 1: (RS) K.

Rows 2–6: K1,*k4, p4; rep from * to last st; then k1.

Row 7: K.

Rows 8–12: K1, *p4, k4; rep from * to last st; then k1.

K 2 rows after st patt.

BO.

The Simple Slip Stitch

This 2-row pattern includes a simple technique of slipping a stitch.

Strong vertical ridges are a feature of the simple slip stitch. The wrong side (right) shows the slipped stitch very clearly.

To slip a stitch, you pass one stitch from the left needle to the right needle without knitting or purling the stitch. You can slip stitches knitwise, with the yarn in back, or purlwise, with the yarn in front.

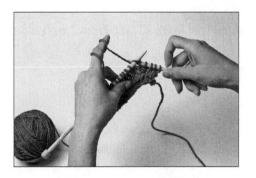

Insert the needle as if to knit from the left of the first stitch.

Slide the stitch from the left to the right needle.

If slipping purlwise, insert the needle from the right of the stitch.

Slide the stitch onto the right needle.

You'll find slipped stitches in parts of patterns where you decrease, change colors, or create smooth selvedge edges. Your pattern will specify if you are to slip knitwise or purlwise.

Swatch It!

(multiples of 4 sts plus 3)

CO 21 sts.

Row 1: (RS) K2, *slip (sl) 1 knitwise (*wyib—with yarn in back*), k3; rep from * to last 3 sts, sl 1 wyib (knitwise), k2.

Row 2: P.

Cont until piece measures 4⅞ inches.

BO.

The Garter Ridges

This 10-row pattern creates horizontal stripes in a combination of stockinette stitch and garter stitch.

You can make garter ridges in many different configurations. They add interest to monochrome pieces and can also be used when changing colors in striping. The wrong side (right) does not have the strength the right side has.

Swatch It!

(any number of stitches)

CO 18 sts.

Row 1: (RS) K.

Row 2: P.

Row 3: K.

Row 4: P.

Rows 5–10: P.

Rep patt until piece measures 4⅞ inches.

BO.

The Broken Rib

In this stitch pattern, multiples of 4 with an extra stitch on each end for selvedge results in a beautiful textured pattern.

This pattern reminds me of tiling and looks great when used in garments.

Swatch It!

(multiples of 4 sts plus 2)

CO 18 sts.

Row 1: (RS) K1, *k2, p2; rep from * last st, k1.

Rows 2–6: Rep Row 1.

Rows 7–12: K1,*p2, k2; rep from * to last st, k1.

Rep patt until piece measures 4⅞ inches.

BO.

The Least You Need to Know

- A selvedge is created by adding 1 or 2 stitches at the beginning and end of each row. This gives the sides of your knitted pieces a firm edge, assists you in counting rows, and makes sewing pieces together easier.

- Reversible patterns are great for scarves, shawls, cuffs, and any pieces where both sides of the piece will show.

- Remember to count your stitches, especially as you learn more complex patterns.

Advanced Stitches

In This Chapter

- Ready for a challenge
- Get ready for a few twists and turns with the bramble stitch
- Diamond brocade—pretty and complex
- The lovely cluster lace
- A perfectly simple cable

Now that you've learned the easy stitches in Chapter 5 and the intermediate stitches in Chapter 6, you're ready for the more complex patterns in this advanced chapter.

The bramble stitch is more three-dimensional. The diamond brocade is an 8-row pattern that creates a diamond-shape design element. The diagonal cluster lace includes a technique wherein you go back and manipulate stitches you've already knitted. And finally, the simple cable shows the basic technique of making cables.

The Bramble Stitch

This stitch is sometimes known as a blackberry stitch. It involves knitting and purling into 1 stitch and then combining stitches together to form a cluster of stitches.

This is a 4-row pattern that gives great texture to a garment, especially along the bottom edge of a sweater or the ends of a shawl.

Swatch It!

(multiples of 4 sts)

CO 24 sts.

Row 1: (RS) P.

Row 2: *[K1, p1, k1] in the same st, *p3tog;* rep from * to end.

Notice the brackets around the first three procedures. These indicate that all 3 stitches are performed in the same stitch.

The bramble, or blackberry, stitch features bold berries and an interesting diagonal pattern. The wrong side of the bramble stitch (right) is quite subdued.

Insert the needle into the first stitch knitwise.

Knit into that stitch, but do not transfer the stitch to the right needle.

Here is the first of the 3 stitches.

Now bring your yarn in front of the needles, and purl into the same stitch.

The knit stitch and the purl stitch are still on the left needle.

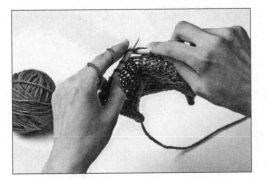

Take the yarn in back of the needles again, and knit 1 more stitch.

Transfer all 3 stitches to the right needle.

Insert the right needle purlwise into the next 3 stitches.

Wrap the yarn around the right needle.

Pull the yarn through on the right needle.

Here are all 3 stitches combined in the p3tog stitch.

 DEFINITION

Knitting or **purling stitches together** is a way of decreasing the number of stitches on your needle. The abbreviation is **k2tog** (knit 2 together), or in the case of the bramble stitch, **p3tog** (purl 3 together).

Row 3: P.

Row 4: *P3tog, [k1, p1, k1] in same st; rep from * to end.

Rep patt until piece measures 4⅞ inches.

BO.

The Diamond Brocade

The diamond brocade is one of those patterns you really need to concentrate on. You might want to turn off your iPod or the TV while you work it. I turn the music off in my head with these kinds of patterns.

Diamonds appear as you complete each group of 8 rows. The purl stitches obscure the diamond pattern a little on the wrong side (right).

The diamond brocade is not difficult, but you need to keep track of where you are within every row and row by row.

Swatch It!

(multiples of 8 sts plus 1)

CO 18 sts.

Row 1: (RS) K4, *p1, k7; rep from * to last 5 sts, p1, k4.

Row 2: P3, *k1, p1, k1, p5; rep from * to last 6 sts, k1, p1, k1, p3.

Row 3: K2, *p1, k3; rep from * to last 3 sts, p1, k2.

Row 4: P1, *k1, p5, k1, p1; rep from * to end.

Row 5: *P1, k7; rep from * to last st, p1.

Row 6: as per Row 4.

Row 7: as per Row 3.

Row 8: as per Row 2.

Rep patt until piece measures 4⅞ inches.

BO.

The Diagonal Cluster Lace

This is one of my favorite patterns. I love the texture, diagonal lines, and open spaces. It's fun to knit and a bit of a challenge. You'll find it used in the Diamond Lace Vest project in Chapter 13.

The diagonal cluster lace pattern is at once lacy, dynamic, and visually interesting. The wrong side (right) looks more complex than the right side (left).

The diagonal cluster lace pattern includes yarn-overs (YO), which adds a stitch and a technique for decreasing a stitch by passing 1 stitch over 2 others.

Bring the yarn around the right needle from front to back.

Insert the left needle in the first of 3 stitches on the right needle.

Pull that stitch over the other 2, leaving 2 stitches of that group on the right needle.

Swatch It!

(multiples of 3 sts)

CO 18 sts.

Row 1: (WS) P.

Row 2: K2, *YO, k3, pass 1st of the 3 knit sts over the 2nd and 3rd sts; rep from * to end, k1. (Do not YO before the last st. If you do, you'll add a st.)

Row 3: P.

Row 4: K1, *k3, pass 1st of the 3 k sts over the 2nd and 3rd sts, YO; rep from * to end, k2. (Remember to YO before the last 2 sts in this row.)

Rep patt until piece measures 4⅞ inches.

BO.

The Simple Cable

This easy cable stitch illustrates why cables are so much fun to knit. When you knit a cable, you're actually knitting stitches out of order and crossing them in the process.

Creating this cable is quite easy. You cross 2 stitches over 2 others in Row 3 of the 4-row pattern. Like a rib pattern, this piece has some elasticity, as you can see from the wrong side of the swatch (right).

You need a third needle or even a pencil to work this pattern. Special cable needles are available, and some people like to use double-pointed needles, but for this swatch, you only need an additional straight needle. Just be sure the tool you use is the same diameter or a little smaller than the needle you're using.

Swatch It!

(multiples of 22 sts)

CO 22 sts.

Row 1: (RS) K4, p5, k4, p5, k4.

Row 2: P4, k5, p4, k5, p4.

Row 3: (This is the cable row.) K4, p5, place the next 2 sts on the 3rd needle (ndl) or cable ndl, k the next 2 sts on the original left ndl, k the 2 sts on the cable ndl (or place the sts on the 3rd ndl back on the left ndl and then k them), p5, k4.

When you get to the middle of the cable row, place the next 2 stitches on the third needle.

Knit the next 2 stitches on the left needle.

Knit the 2 stitches on the cable needle. Some knitters like to place these stitches back on the left needle and then knit them.

Your 4-stitch cable is complete.

Row 4: as per Row 2.

Rep patt until piece measures 4⅞ inches.

BO.

There are so many, many more patterns to explore. You'll find them in books, online, and in the clothes you buy. Hopefully, you'll try a great number of them as you continue your knitting journey.

The Least You Need to Know

- Knitting or purling stitches together is one technique for decreasing the number of stitches in a row.
- A yarn-over adds a stitch.
- Brackets around a set of instructions indicate that all of the procedures are done in the same stitch.

Mini Fifteen-Block Sampler

In This Chapter

- Your first sampler
- Block by block—your swatch collection
- Garter and stockinette swatches
- Assembling your sampler

If you've been following along with the preceding chapters, you now know how to make all the easy, intermediate, and advanced knit stitch patterns—congratulations!

You also should have accumulated a small pile of swatches as you practiced the stitches in the earlier chapters. Rather than toss those, or let them loiter in your knitting basket, let's put them to use in a sampler. This project will be a testament to what you've learned so far, from the basic stitches to the more advanced stitch patterns you've conquered.

Building Your Sampler

Okay, gather your swatches, and let's review what you should have by now.

In Chapter 5, you started off with the easy stitches:

- The seed stitch
- The moss stitch
- The purl ridges stitch
- The 2×2 rib stitch

In Chapter 6, you tackled the intermediate stitches:

- The mock rib stitch

- The basket weave stitch

- The simple slip stitch

- The garter ridges stitch

- The broken rib stitch

In Chapter 7, you took on the advanced stitches:

- The bramble stitch

- The diamond brocade stitch

- The diagonal cluster lace stitch

- The simple cable stitch

We looked at the garter stitch in Chapter 2 and the stockinette stitch in Chapter 3, so that should round out your group of 15 swatch blocks.

JAZZING IT UP

Each stitch pattern block is a 5×5-inch square. If you prefer to make a throw for this practice project, double the number of pattern stitches and make each square 10 inches wide and 10 inches high. Be sure to check each pattern, though. If a pattern has additional stitches, don't double those stitches. For example, the basket weave stitch is multiples of 8 plus 2. You'd double the 8 but not the 2 additional stitches.

Take a good look at your swatches. Now that you're more proficient, you may want to knit a few of them over again. Your gauge has probably changed, and you have better control over the evenness of your stitches. You may want to change yarns or vary the colors.

Garter Stitch and Stockinette Blocks

You learned these stitches in Chapters 2 and 3, and the swatches you made then should be part of your 15-block sampler. If you didn't make the swatches then, don't worry. I give you the instructions for those first two swatches here. (And if you did already make them and those early attempts look a little rough compared to your later, more practiced stitches, feel free to knit them over again. I won't tell.)

Don't forget to check your gauge so each square is 5×5 inches!

The Garter Stitch

The most simple of all stitch patterns, the garter stitch is a favorite of experienced and new knitters alike.

The garter stitch can accommodate any number of stitches because you're just repeating the same stitch over and over. The knitted fabric will be somewhat elastic yet sturdy. The edges won't roll like they do with the stockinette stitch, and both sides look exactly the same.

Swatch It!

(any number of sts)

CO 16 sts.

Row 1: K all sts.

Rep Row 1 until piece measures 4⅞ inches.

BO.

The Stockinette Stitch

The stockinette stitch is one of the most common and popular stitches you'll find. It's a 2-row pattern with 1 row all knit (that's the right side) and the other row all purl (that's the wrong side). Smooth on the knit side and bumpy on the purl side, stockinette is also known as the *stocking stitch* because it's the stitch used to knit stockings!

After making your swatch, you'll notice that the sides curve toward the back. This curled edge can work to your advantage if you want this kind of decorative edge. The curling is caused by the tension between the knitted stitches on one side and the purl stitches on the other. In some patterns where a flat edge is needed, a selvedge edge of 1 or 2 stitches is recommended.

Look at the back or wrong side (WS). Patterns that call for the purl side as the right side (RS) are called reverse stockinette stitch.

Swatch It!

(any number of sts)

CO 18 sts.

Row 1: (RS) K all sts.

Row 2: (WS) P all sts.

Rep Rows 1 and 2 until piece measures 4⅞ inches.

BO in st patt.

Assembling Your Sampler

All you need to assemble your sampler is some leftover yarn from your swatches, a large-eye darning needle, and scissors.

Here's how to put it all together:

1. Lay out all the pieces on a table with right sides up.

2. Take a look at those with curling edges like the stockinette swatch. Move these swatches to the inside positions so they won't curl up on the edge of the sampler.

3. Place the swatches with the firm edges in the outside positions.

4. Arrange your swatches in 3 horizontal or vertical rows—your choice.

5. When you have a design you like, turn over all the swatches so the wrong sides are now up.

6. Beginning at one of the corners, whipstitch the edges of two swatches together.

7. Continue sewing up the contiguous edges until all your swatches are joined together.

8. Turn right side up and enjoy.

You can use this sampler as a wall hanging, make it into a pillow, or use it as a placemat. If you're feeling really ambitious, you can knit all the swatches larger and assemble them into a blanket!

This fun sampler is a great way to document your knitting progress as you learn each stitch pattern.

The Least You Need to Know

- As you become more proficient, your stitches will be more even and your gauge will improve.
- The sampler is a wonderful record of your stitch patterns and the beginning of your knitting experience.
- The whipstitch is a great way to sew edges together.

Shaping, Knitting in the Round, and More

In Part 3, we explore adding stitches, deleting stitches, knitting stitches in the round, and knitting colorful stitches. There are many ways of increasing and decreasing the number of stitches on your needles. This is called shaping, and it's essential to making garments fit well.

To knit in the round, you can use circular or double-pointed needles. You learn the uses and techniques for both kinds of tools in Part 3 and then move on to making bags, hats, sweaters, and other three-dimensional projects.

Knitting with lots of colors can increase your enjoyment of the craft. I give you plenty of tips for knowing when and how to change colors for simple stripes in the following chapters.

Also in Part 3, you learn how to read a pattern and practice the techniques you've learned so far in projects ranging from a baby blanket and beret to a great little handbag.

Increasing and Decreasing

In This Chapter

- Overview of shaping techniques
- Increasing—ways of adding stitches
- Decreasing—taking away stitches

Sure, knitting flat, square and rectangle pieces with straight edges is fine, but that will get boring after a while. That's where shaping comes in. You'll find shaping quite easy.

With increases and decreases you will be able to make shapes, tailor garments so they fit properly, and work in three dimensions. When you add stitches, you are increasing. When you combine stitches, you are decreasing. Each technique will have a different visual effect.

Increasing

In preparation for learning these techniques, let's begin a swatch with your practice yarn and needles.

Swatch It!

CO 10 sts and k 2 rows.

Cont stockinette st for 4 more rows (k 1 row, p 1 row, rep).

This is a good place to begin learning your increase techniques.

The Bar Increase (or Knit Into Front and Back of Stitch—kf&b)

This technique is a very common way of adding a single stitch to a garment or hat. In patterns, you may see it as a bar increase because it creates a visual bar where the additional stitch is added. It's also referred to as knitting into the front and back of the stitch (kf&b).

Here's how you do it:

1. K3 in the next row.

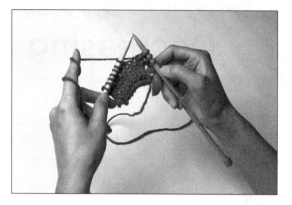

2. Now k into the next st, and keep it on the left ndl. Do not let it slide off.

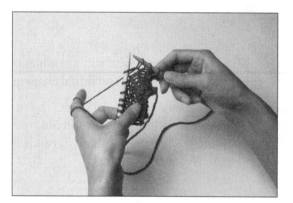

3. Next, put your ndl through the front of the same st, angling it toward the back, and bring forward an additional st. There will be 2 sts on your right ndl coming from the original st on the left ndl.

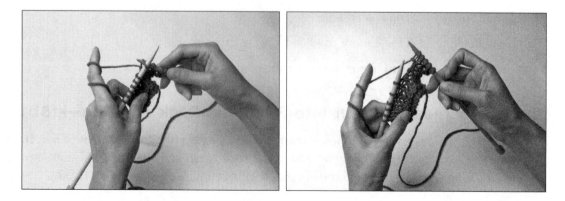

4. Look at the bar under the last st. It's right above the new st.

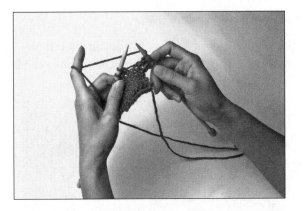

5. Cont k the row of sts, and p back. You now have 11 sts and are ready to try the next technique on the knit side.

Yarn-Over (YO) Increases, Knitwise and Purlwise

I love yarn-overs. With each yarn-over, you create a hole, which is why yarn-overs are often used in lace patterns. You can yarn-over knitwise and yarn-over purlwise, and we try both in this section.

Yarn-over knitwise:

1. K3. Now bring the working yarn around your right ndl before knitting the next st. The yarn comes around from the back to the front and over the ndl, ready to k the next st on your left ndl.

2. K the next 4 sts on the left ndl.

3. YO knitwise once more, and k to the end of the row. You should now have 13 sts.

4. P the next row, including the new YO sts. Look at the right side (RS) and the holes left by the YO.

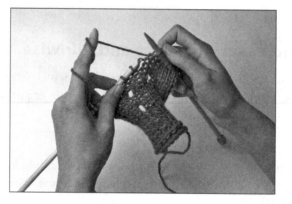

Yarn-over purlwise:

5. K the next row so we can try it purlwise.

6. With the ndl with the sts in your left hand, you should be looking at the purl side. P4. Wrap the yarn around your right ndl from the front to the back.

7. P the next 5 sts.

8. YO purlwise once more, and p to the end of the row. You should now have 15 sts. Again, look at the RS and note the holes in the sample.

9. K the next row, including the YOs.

10. Cont for 2 more rows of stockinette, ending with the right side (RS) ready for the next row.

Make One (m1)

You'll often find patterns that instruct you to "make one" (m1). With this technique, you add a stitch that either slants right or left. Why is this important? Because when you're shaping a garment, for instance, you want your increased stitches to be consistently going in one direction or another, slanting to the right or left. To demonstrate this, let's do a few rows in our swatch.

Make 1 right slanting—knit side:

1. K5. Now make 1 by picking up the horizontal strand with your left ndl from back to front between the last st on the right ndl and the next st on the left ndl.

2. K that new st on the left ndl from the front.

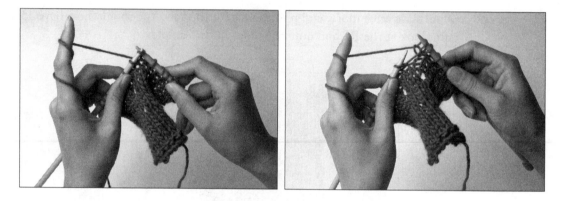

3. K to the end. You now have 16 sts.

Make 1 right slanting—purl side:

1. P5. Now make 1 by picking up the horizontal strand with the left ndl from back to front between the last st on the right ndl and the next st on the left ndl.

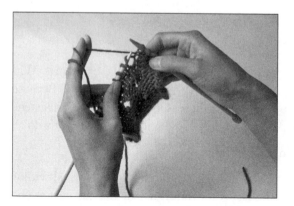

2. P that new st.

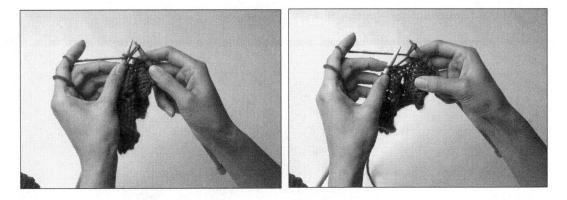

3. P to the end. You now have 17 sts.

4. K 1 row, and p 1 row.

Make 1 left slanting—knit side:

1. K5. Make 1 by picking up the horizontal strand with the left ndl from front to back.

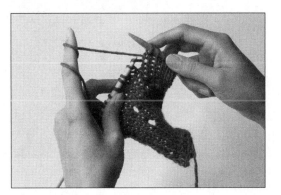

2. K the new st on the left ndl.

3. K to the end of the row (18 sts).

Make 1 left slanting—purl side:

1. P5. Make 1 by picking up the horizontal strand with the left ndl from front to back.

2. P the new st on the left ndl.

3. P to the end of the row (17 sts).

Decreasing

When you need to reduce the number of stitches, you can use several methods. Sometimes it's just a matter of binding off stitches. Other techniques include knitting or purling stitches together or slipping one stitch over another.

Let's continue working with our practice sample. At the end of the increase section, you ended up with 17 stitches. Now we'll decrease some of those stitches using these techniques.

Knitting (k2tog) or Purling Stitches Together (p2tog)

Knit 2 together, or purl 2 together, is one of the most common ways of decreasing. The technique is quite simple. You simply insert your needle into 2 stitches at the same time and either knit or purl them together.

Swatch It!

K7.

Insert your right ndl into the next 2 sts from the left of the 2nd st.

K2tog.

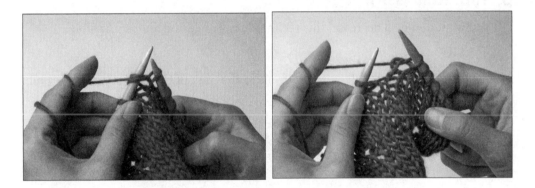

K the remaining sts in the row (16 sts remain).

Cont with stockinette for 3 rows.

On the next row (WS), p7.

Insert your right ndl into the next 2 sts from the right of the 1st st.

P2tog.

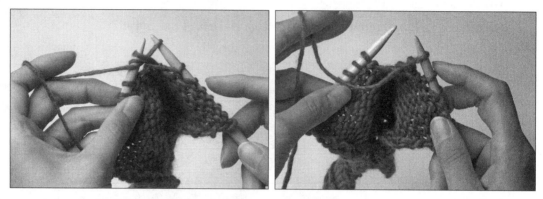

P the remaining sts in the row (15 sts remain).

Cont with stockinette st for 3 more rows.

Slip, Slip, Knit (ssk)

If you want to hide a decrease, this technique is simple and almost invisible.

1. K4.

2. Insert the right ndl from the front to the back of the next st on the left ndl, and slip it onto the right ndl.

3. Slip the next st the same way.

4. Insert the left ndl into the fronts of both of the slipped sts, and k together.

5. K to the end of the row.

6. P the next row.

Slip 1, Knit 1, Pass Slipped Stitch Over (sk psso)

Passing a slipped stitch over sounds complicated, but it really isn't:

1. K6.

2. Slip the next st from the left to the right ndl.

3. K the next st.

4. Using the left ndl, grab the slipped st and pull it over the point of the right ndl and over the k st. K to end of row.

Knit to the end of the row, and bind off the next row. You may want to keep this swatch for reference.

Project: Fortune Cookie Hooded Baby Blanket

If you're *fortune*-ate to have a cute little "cookie" in your life, he or she will love wrapping up in this soft, cozy hooded blanket.

This cotton baby wrap is perfect for cool days.

This blanket is knit on the bias, giving you plenty of opportunity to practice your increasing and decreasing. You can either make this piece in one color, or you can design a pattern of stripes. Simply introduce a different color when a ball is finished and you need to start the new ball. Just be sure you add your new ball or color at the beginning of the right side row.

Finished size:

> 26×26 inches (If you make it larger, you can work it up as a wonderful lap blanket or afghan.)

Materials:

> 3 skeins Lion Brand Cotton-Ease 100g, 207 yards/skein, 50 percent cotton, 50 percent acrylic machine washable and dryable in color of your choice
>
> To make in the same colors as the model, use 1 skein each Lime (color 194), Sand (color 098), and Maize (color 186)
>
> U.S. 8 (5mm) 24-inch circular needle
>
> 2 removable stitch markers

Gauge:

> Not critical

Stitch pattern:

> *Garter stitch:* K every st, every row

Abbreviations:

k2tog	knit 2 together
kf&b	knit into front and back of stitch
m1l	make 1 left slanting
m1r	make 1 right slanting
p2tog	purl 2 together
sk psso	slip 1, knit 1, pass slipped stitch over
ssk	slip, slip, knit
YO	yarn-over

JAZZING IT UP

Changing to a new skein or color is simple. When you've finished a Row 2 (WS) on the increase or decrease side of the blanket and don't think you have enough yarn to work another row, start a Row 1 with a new skein of yarn. If you're changing colors, this is the time to do it. All color changes begin on a Row 1. When looking at the Row 2 side of the blanket where a color change occurs, the stitches will be half one color and half the other colors. On the right side (RS), it's a seamless transition.

Basic square knit on the bias:

The blanket starts out as a basic square, knit on the bias. The hood is added later by adding a simple triangle.

CO 3 sts.

Row 1: (WS) K1, m1r, k1, m1l, k1.

Row 2: (RS) K all sts.

Work these 2 rows one time.

Increase pattern rows:

Row 3: K1, m1r, k across row to last st, m1l, k1.

Row 4: K all sts.

To keep track of the increase side, place removable stitch markers at the beginning and end of the work on a Row 1 side (WS). Garter stitch is reversible, so it's easy to forget which is the Row 1 side unless you mark it. As the rows begin to have more and more stitches, the marker at the beginning and end of a Row 1 serve as a reminder to make the increases. Continue to move the markers up as the work continues to grow, and you can keep them easily in view.

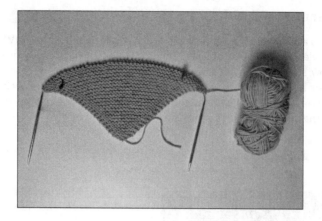

Continue to knit the 2 increase pattern rows until the sides of the blanket measure 26 inches from the CO to the needle. (The sample has 139 stitches at the point.) Then begin the decrease rows on the WS.

Decrease pattern rows:

Row 5: K1, ssk, k across row to last 3 sts, k2tog, k1.

Row 6: K all sts.

Follow the dec patt rows until 3 sts remain, and finish with a Row 2.

K3tog.

BO, cut the yarn, and pull the end through the last st.

Hood:

Begin the hood following the same directions as for the blanket, and continue with the same increases until the sides from the CO to the needle measure 8 inches. You'll be increasing evenly on both sides, creating a triangle of approximately 49 stitches.

BO all st.

Fasten off, leaving a 2-yard length of yarn for attaching the hood to the blanket.

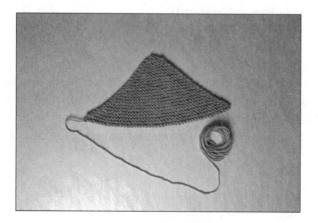

Assembly:

Weave in all tails in their corresponding colors.

Place the blanket in front of you with obvious color change rows facing you (WS facing you). Place the hood over the blanket corner of the same color. Thread a tapestry needle or a large-eye darning needle with the tail from the bind-off. Whipstitch the edges of the hood and the blanket together.

Weave in the yarn tail for a couple inches, and fasten off. This blanket will be machine washed and dried, so be sure your tails are well secured.

The Least You Need to Know

- You can increase, or add stitches, in several ways, including yarn-overs, knitting into the back and front of a single stitch, and the bar increase.
- Knitting stitches together and binding off are two ways to decrease, or reduce the number of stitches.
- Increasing and decreasing enable you to create shapes, tailor garments, and work in three dimensions.

Knitting in the Round

In This Chapter

- Knitting in the round
- Working with circular needles
- Working with double-pointed needles
- Making an I-cord

Up to this point, you've been knitting flat, two-dimensional pieces. But in this chapter, we explore working in three dimensions by working in the round. This technique can be used for many purposes, including bags, sleeves, socks, hats, and even the bottom half of sweaters.

Knitting in the round reduces or eliminates the number of seams in a project. Your work progresses by "rounds" instead of rows, with the right side (RS) of your work facing you. If you're working the stockinette stitch, you will knit every round without ever purling.

Knitting in Circles

There are two ways of knitting in the round:

- Working with a circular needle
- Working with double-pointed needles

Knitting with Circular Needles (cir)

Circular needles are designed with two straight, short needles attached to a flexible cable or tubing. They're available in standard needle sizes and in lengths from 8 to 47 inches. For those who love making socks, there is even now a circular needle small enough for socks! Instructions will specify the length you need based on the number of stitches in the pattern.

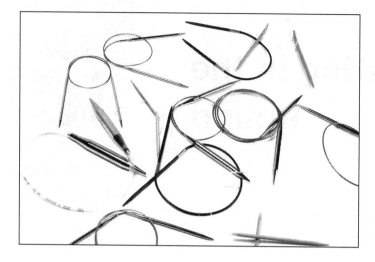

The needle part of a circular needle can be made of metal, bamboo, wood, or plastic and come in all sizes.

Circular needles are also wonderful for straight knitting, especially when you're working with lots of stitches. You can make an entire afghan on circular needles, turning your work and knitting back and forth. This eliminates sewing strips or sections together later.

The main lesson to learn when using circular needles is right at the beginning of the process. After you cast on your stitches, you join the first stitch in the round to the last stitch in the round. The trick is to be sure all your stitches are straight, laying in the same direction. If your row of stitches is twisted at any point, you'll have to begin your round over.

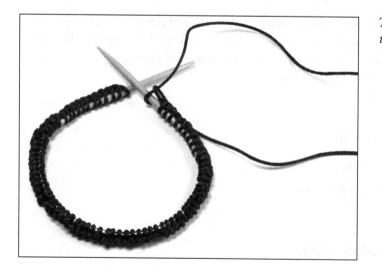

The stitches on this circular are all laying in the same direction, ready to be joined together.

Notice the arrow pointing to the twist. If you joined the circle together, your knitting would be tangled and you'd have to start over.

You will be placing a stitch marker on the needle at the beginning of the round. (You can also just use a piece of contrasting yarn tied in a loop if you don't have stitch markers.)

As you knit, the marker will move around the needle and serve as your guide to the next round. Patterns will indicate *PM* for "place marker."

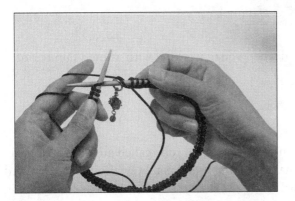

Placing a marker at the beginning of a round helps you as you knit your pattern.

Knitting with Double-Pointed Needles (dpn)

Double-pointed needles are available in the same sizes as straight needles and come in packages of five. The concept is to put stitches on three or four of the needles and use a fourth or fifth needle to knit the stitches. As you knit the stitches on each needle, you free another needle to work with.

When a pattern calls for knitting in the round with three needles, you'll use a fourth needle to work the stitches.

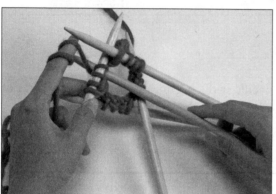

When knitting in the round with four double-pointed needles, you use the fifth to work the stitches.

Double-pointed needles are primarily used when you're working with a small number of stitches.

Making an I-Cord

Using two double-pointed needles, you can create a knitted tube called an I-cord. According to Montse Stanley's *Knitter's Handbook*, the name *I-cord* is a polite abbreviation for "idiot cord," but I prefer to think of it as "inspirational cord."

You can make so many things with I-cords: bag handles, headbands, necklaces, belts, rugs, surface embellishments, and trims, to name just a few. You also can create patterns with different stitch combinations and change colors and textures, depending on your project.

Begin with two double-pointed needles, size U.S. 10 or 10.5.

1. CO 4 sts on 1 ndl.

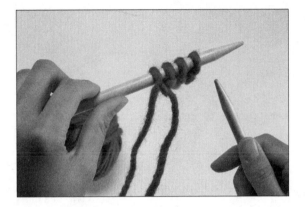

2. *K4, pulling the yarn around from the back left to the front right of the sts.

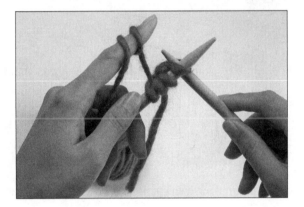

3. Pull the tail downward; do not turn your work.

4. Slide the sts to the other end of the ndl. The working yarn will be on your left.

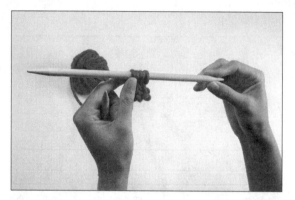

5. Rep steps 2 and 3 until you have your desired length.

Remember to pull the tail down after every row or two to set the stitches.

Project: Little Black Bag

Our BagSmith Little Black Bag is one of our most popular purse kits. The kit includes all you need to make the bag, including a liner. This bag works up quickly and is a great weekend project. You can finish the bag using the enclosed handles, or you can knit an I-cord for a shoulder strap. (For more information about purchasing the kit from BagSmith, see Appendix B.)

You begin with the body of the bag, which is a 6-inch-high tube worked on circular needles. The patches used to hold the handles are worked on the same needles, but in straight fashion, back and forth. You'll need double-pointed needles if you choose to make the I-cord strap.

The little black bag is the perfect accessory for day or night. It works up so quickly, you can complete it over a weekend.

The kit includes everything you need: a nylon cord, handles, a baseboard, drawstring liner, and a beaded button.

Finished size:

6 inches H×6 inches W×4 inches D

Materials:

BagSmith Little Black Bag Kit (175 yards nylon cord, 2 handles, drawstring liner, beaded button, baseboard bottom)

U.S. 7 (4.5mm) 16- or 20-inch circular needle (I prefer the 20-inch length. The stitches are easier to work on the longer needle.)

U.S. 7 (4.5mm) double-pointed needles for optional I-cord shoulder strap

Stitch marker

Large-eye darning needle

U.S. I crochet hook (Crochet hooks are listed with letter sizes or metric measurements.)

Long straight pins

Gauge:

Seed stitch: 4 sts = 1 inch; 7 rows = 1 inch

Garter stitch: 5 sts = 1 inch; 7 rows = 1 inch

Stitch pattern:

Seed stitch:

Rnd 1: *K1, p1; rep to end of rnd.

Rnd 2: *P1, k1; rep to end of rnd.

Garter stitch: K every rnd.

Abbreviations:

cir	circular or circle
cont	continue
dpn	double-pointed needle
ndl	needle
patt	pattern
PM	place a stitch marker
rnd	round

Body of bag:

CO 77 sts on cir ndl. PM at st near working yarn.

Rnd 1: Begin knitting into last st of CO, and continue with seed st patt. Be sure your sts aren't twisted.

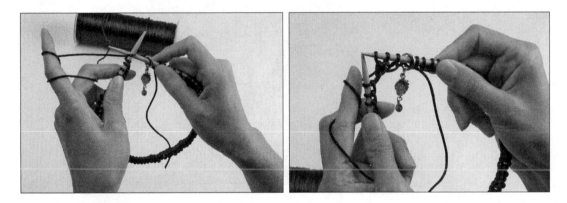

Rnd 2: *P1, k1; rep to end of rnd.

Cont working in the round until the piece (tube) measures 6 inches high.

BO in st patt until 11 sts remain on ndl. This begins the closure flap.

Now work back and forth in seed st for 7 rows.

Decrease rows:

*BO 1 st at beg of row, and k2tog at end of row; rep until 3 sts remain.

Cut the cord, leaving a 24-inch tail. Insert the crochet hook into the 3 sts.

Draw the tail through the remaining sts.

Using the crochet hook, draw up a loop using the tail near the last knit st and cont making a 3-inch chain. To do this, insert the hook into the last st, YO on the hook, and pull it through, leaving it on the hook. Rep.

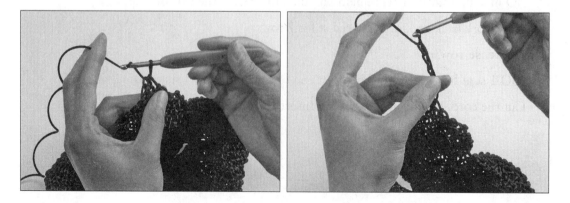

Attach the tail to the inside part of the flap, creating a loop. Knot securely, and wind in the end.

Fold over flap, and position the button so the loop on the flap lines up.

Using the cord, sew the button in place, and knot the yarn securely.

Handles (make 2):

CO 18 sts.

K 12 rows, and BO.

Center the rectangle under the flap inside the tube, and whipstitch the bottom edge. Do not cut the cord.

Set the handle in place, and sew the top edge.

Rep on the opposite side.

Bottom of bag:

CO 25 sts on cir ndl.

Using garter st, continue for 30 rows or until piece measures 4 inches. This is a flat piece for the bottom of the bag.

BO, leaving a 30-inch tail.

Whipstitch knitted rectangle to baseboard through holes.

Pin baseboard in place at bottom of the tube. Be sure the corners are parallel to the handles and the corners line up correctly.

Whipstitch around the baseboard, attaching it to body.

Optional I-cord strap:

On dpn, CO 5 sts.

K I-cord patt until piece measures 36 inches long.

Attach each end to the side walls of the bag.

You can knit along an additional thin yarn with the cord or embellish your bag after you knit it. The possibilities are endless for a one-of-a-kind masterpiece.

JAZZING IT UP

The Little Black Bag was featured on a segment of *Needle Arts Studio* with Shay Pendray. The segment shows how to make the bag and embellish it to create a one-of-a-kind accessory. View the segment on BagSmith's YouTube channel, www.youtube.com/watch?v=esp7sPD2jHE.

The Least You Need to Know

- Knitting in the round is a great way to make bags, socks, hats, and parts of garments. It eliminates the need to sew seams together.
- Circular needles come in all sizes and in wood, bamboo, metal, and plastic with cables in a variety of lengths.
- Double-pointed needles are available in all sizes and materials.
- Ensuring that your stitches aren't twisted when beginning to join the round is one of the most important things to remember about circular knitting.

Changing Colors

In This Chapter

- Adding color to your projects
- Changing colors—where and when
- Creating a firm foundation row with cable cast-on

Changing colors can add excitement and interest to your projects. Stripes and color blocks are easily achieved and can give your project punch. Master knitters like Kaffe Fassett use color in marvelous ways, creating unusual shapes that can simulate nature.

In this chapter, we explore color changes as well as a new cast-on technique called cable cast-on. This technique provides a firm cast-on edge, good for hats and other items where elasticity isn't wanted.

Where and How to Add the Next Color

Patterns are usually very specific about where and when to change colors. The colors are given letter designations (A, B, C, etc.), and the pattern tells you which color you need to switch out by the appropriate letter. If you're changing colors back and forth within a few stitches, you don't have to cut the yarn. Instead, you carry it in the back (on the wrong side) as you continue knitting with the new color. If you're going to be using a color for several rows, you can cut the yarn, leaving enough of a tail to wind it into the fabric.

If you're creating a garment that has wide stripes, it's best to change yarns at the end of the row, leaving the tails to wind in later. If your stripes are short and thin, you can leave one color attached and exchange it later. You can incorporate the slack along the edge into the seam of the garment. Use your best judgment in situations where the pattern doesn't specify what to do.

The practice project in this chapter is a beret knit in the round. When you're changing yarns in the round, tie a loose overhand knot with the tails of the two yarns. Later, if the knots are too bulky, undo the knots and weave the tails into stitches of their respective colors.

Cable Cast-On

The cable cast-on gives you a very sturdy series of foundation stitches and is a good way to begin a piece that needs less elasticity or a firm addition of stitches to an existing project.

1. Using the long-tail or simple CO, put 2 sts on the left ndl.

2. Insert the right ndl between the 2 sts from front to back.

3. Wrap the yarn around the ndl.

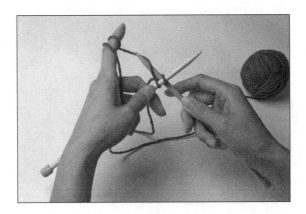

4. Pull the yarn through, between the 2 sts, forming a loop.

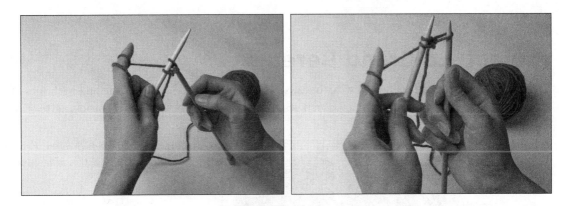

5. Lift the loop over the point of the left ndl.

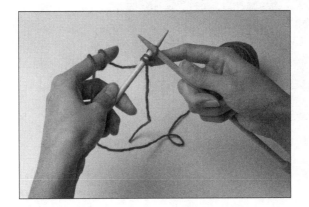

6. Rest the new st near the point of the left ndl. Your right ndl should now be empty.

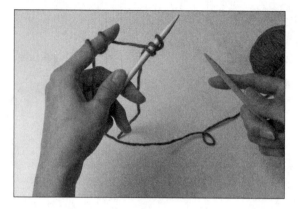

7. Rep for the desired number of sts, always putting the right ndl between the st closest to the point and the next st.

Project: Le Grand Beret

This oversize beret is fun to wear because you can put it in several positions with lots of attitude. The brim is knitted in a 2×2 rib stitch pattern, and the body is all stockinette stitch.

This beret calls for four colors. Each yarn provides a slightly different texture.

You begin the pattern with the circular needle, and after the first few sections of the decrease area in the crown, you transfer the stitches to double-pointed needles (dpn).

Finished size:

11 (12) inches in diameter (Measure with the piece flat on a table.)

Materials:

U.S. 10.5 (6.5mm) 24-inch circular needles

U.S. 10.5 double-pointed needles (Adjust needle size to obtain the correct gauge.)

Coloratura Yarns, Fine Merino Flecks; 10 percent rayon flecks, 90 percent merino wool; 85 yards per skein; 1.75 ounces (50 grams); 1 skein each of Orange (color A) and Tomato (color C)

Coloratura Yarns, Glitter Wiggles; 90 percent Columbia Wool, 10 percent polyester wound with one silver and one gold metallic thread; 85 yards per skein; 1.75 ounces (50 grams); 1 skein each of Brass (color B) and Orange (color D)

Stitch marker

Large-eye darning needle

Gauge:

3.5 sts = 1 inch; 5 rows = 1 inch

Brim (2×2 rib):

Beg with color A and the circular ndl.

CO 64 (76) sts, and work in the round. PM at the beg of the rnd.

UNRAVELING

Be sure you move the stitch marker into the new round as you knit. This helps you keep your place, especially as you increase and decrease.

Rnd 1: *K2, p2; rep from * to end of rnd.

Rnds 2–8: Rep Rnd 1. This should give you a brim of about 1½ inches.

Body (stockinette stitch):

Rnd 9: K all sts for remaining rnds.

Increase row:

Rnd 10: *K1, k1f&b; rep to end of rnd (96, 114 sts).

Rnds 11–16: K.

Rnds 17–22: Change to color B.

Hold the end of color A with the end of color B together in your right hand.

Loosely make an overhand knot. Later, you'll want to release the knot and wind the ends into their respective stripes.

Begin knitting with color B.

Rnds 23–27: Change to color C.

Rnds 28–33: Change to color D.

Decrease rows:

Rnd 34: Change to color A, and k rnd. K all even rows from this point on.

Rnd 35: *K4, k2tog; rep from * to end (80, 95 sts).

Rnd 37: *K3, k2tog; rep from * to end (64, 76 sts).

Rnd 39: *K2, k2tog; rep from * to end (48, 57 sts).

Change to 3 dpns for smaller size. Put 16 sts on each ndl.

Use a 4th ndl to knit off sts.

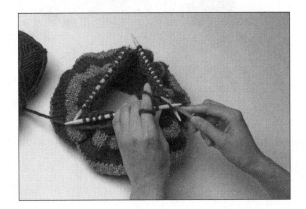

UNRAVELING

Be very careful as you work with the double points. Watch that your stitches don't fall off the ends. If you're concerned, use point protectors at the ends, especially in the first few rows when you have a lot of stitches on the needles.

Finishing smaller size:

Rnd 41: *K2tog; rep from * to end (36 sts). Remember to k all even rows.

Rnd 43: *K2tog; rep from * to end (16 sts).

Rnd 45: Rep Rnd 43 (8 sts), and put all sts on 1 needle.

Cut the yarn, leaving an 8-inch tail, and thread the tail onto the darning needle. Insert the tail through the remaining sts, beginning with the last st on the needle.

Pull the yarn tightly, and knot it close to the beret.

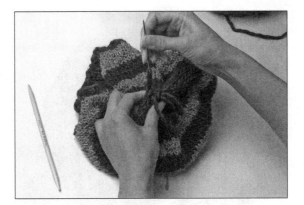

Thread the tail through the top to the inside of the beret.

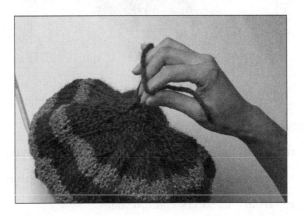

Weave in and out of a few sts, knot, and weave in ends.

The inside of the beret will have many knots, depending on the number of times you changed colors. If the knots where you joined are too bulky, untie them and weave the tails into like-colored stitches.

Finishing larger size:

Rnd 41: *K1, k2tog; rep from * to end (39 sts). Remember to k all even rows.

Change to 3 dpns for larger size. Put 13 sts on each ndl. Use the 4th ndl to knit off.

Rnd 42: *K1, k2tog; rep from * to end of rnd (26 sts).

Rnd 43: *K2tog; rep from * to end of rnd (13 sts).

Rnd 45: *K2tog; rep from * to last st, and put remaining 7 sts on 1 ndl.

Cut the yarn, leaving an 8-inch tail, and thread the tail onto the darning needle. Insert the tail through the remaining sts, beginning with the last st on the needle.

Thread the tail through the top to the inside of the hat. Weave in and out of a few sts, knot, and weave in the end.

JAZZING IT UP

This beret is designed with four colors, but you can easily make it with a fewer or greater number of shades. Just work out the number of rounds you'd like to assign to each color in your design, and keep the rest of the pattern as is.

The Least You Need to Know

- Changing colors can add wonderful interest to your knitting.
- When working on a flat piece with stripes, change colors at the beginning of a row.
- When changing colors in the middle of a row or round, tie a loose knot to be released so you can weave in the ends during finishing.
- The cable cast-on technique is useful when you want a sturdy, less-elastic cast-on.

Intermediate Techniques

Part 4 covers a lot of territory. Shaping your work for great fit, working with enormous needles, controlling multiple yarns, joining the sock craze, and learning how to assemble a sweater—these are all explored in Part 4.

When you knit a sweater that fits well, you'll wear it often with a sense of pride and accomplishment. A good fit depends on many elements: body measurements, appropriate yarn and needles, gauge, and shaping. Graduated shoulder bind-off and three-needle bind-off techniques are covered in Part 4, along with information on swatching with your yarn before starting your project.

Many projects include special edgings and picking up stitches for collars or cuffs. Learning how to pick up stitches makes adding these additions a snap.

Working with needles of various sizes brings enormously different results. In the following chapters, you learn to work with size 2 needles and very thin yarn in sock construction and size 35 and 50 needles and super-bulky and multiple yarns for big stitch knitting.

Finally, assembling a major project like a jacket may seem daunting, but we tackle it like a group of puzzle pieces. A systematic approach to seaming and finishing will make future projects a breeze. Practice projects throughout this part help you work on all these techniques and result in everything from socks to sweaters to rugs.

Simple Shaping

In This Chapter

- The importance of gauge
- Figuring your gauge, sizes, and shaping
- Shoulder shaping
- Dropped stitch pattern

No matter how many years of experience you have knitting, figuring out your gauge should never be a guessing game. Accurately determining your gauge for a garment is critical for your success, so taking the time to work with the specified yarn and needles is essential.

If your yarn is smooth and the thickness is consistent and doesn't vary, a 4×4-inch swatch is usually sufficient to determine if you need to adjust your needle size. If you're working with a thick and thin yarn, or one that changes thicknesses quite often, a larger swatch may be necessary. Whatever the situation, take the time to knit a swatch and check the number of stitches per inch and rows per inch.

Getting Personal with Gauge

I've mentioned gauge several times already, but let's look at it once more, because now's when it really becomes important.

Every knitting pattern includes the details for gauge. You'll also find this information on yarn labels. Preparing a gauge swatch to match those details is very important. If you take the time to do it, you'll save time in the end. Trust me.

The Importance of Figuring Gauge

If you're knitting an afghan and your dimensions are a little bigger or a little smaller than the pattern specifies, it probably won't matter much. An afghan that's 32 inches wide by 61 inches long instead of 30×60 inches is still perfectly usable.

Not so when you're making a garment, however. If a sweater is an inch or two too wide, it won't fit properly. So many knitters I know have made sweaters that are either too big or too small. Taking the time to calculate the accurate number of stitches and rows per inch guarantees that the hours you invest will yield great results.

The most important thing to remember about gauge is this: *it's personal!* Give 10 knitters the same needle and yarn, and they will knit at least 4 different gauge measurements. Some will knit tightly; others, more loosely. I used to think I knitted "to gauge," but I realized many years ago that there's no such thing. The designers who write patterns may not knit at the same gauge you do.

Matching Gauge

Matching a specified gauge is quite simple. Begin with the recommended needle size for the yarn you've chosen. Cast on enough stitches for a swatch 4 inches wide, and work the stitch pattern for the project. When your swatch is about 4 inches long, measure the stitches and rows per inch.

If your gauge is too big (too few stitches per inch), try it again with smaller needles. If your gauge is smaller than the prescribed gauge (too many stitches per inch), work with a larger needle.

There is no "correct needle size," only a correct gauge. When you go to buy a pair of shoes, you want a proper fit. If the style you want fits perfectly in a larger or smaller size than you normally wear, who cares what size it is?

Swatch It!

Here are three swatches worked with the same yarn on three different-size needles. Each swatch has 20 stitches across and is knit to a length of 4 inches. Note that the gauge is measured in the center of the swatch on a flat, even surface. Note, too, you might need to measure the gauge in fractions of stitches. Confirm your gauge by measuring again in another section of the swatch.

This swatch was knitted on size 11 needles. The gauge is 3¹⁄₂ stitches per inch and 6 rows per inch. (Remember, each visible row in garter stitch represents 2 rows of knitting.) The dimensions for the swatch are 5 inches wide by 4 inches high.

This swatch was knitted on size 10.5 needles. The gauge is 4 stitches per inch and 8 rows per inch. The swatch dimensions are 4¹/₂ inches wide by 4 inches high.

The final swatch was worked on size 9 needles. The gauge is 4¹/₂ stitches per inch and 10 rows per inch. The swatch dimensions are 4¹/₂ inches wide by 4 inches high.

If a pattern is written for a specific yarn and you can't find it or don't like it, be sure the yarn you choose will work up in the correct gauge. Otherwise, the pattern won't knit up correctly. Swatch it to ensure your yarn substitution works for you.

Shoulder Shaping

Shaping a shoulder on a sweater allows for a lovely transition, especially if it's a cap or short sleeve. The shaping is accomplished by binding off stitches in steps.

There's really not much to shoulder shaping, and it produces lovely results. The trick is to bind off evenly so that when you match up the shoulders for the seam, the stitches don't pull.

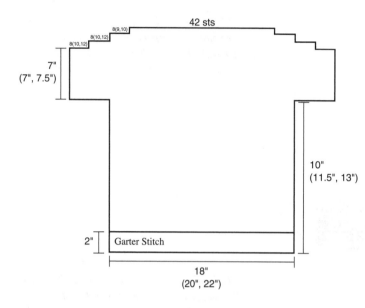

Schematics can be wonderful guides. They visually tell you the dimensions and where the shaping will take place. You'll probably find yourself referring to them regularly, as I do.

Project: My Favorite T

This project gives you a chance to create a knitted T-shirt specifically to the size you want.

Begin by choosing a yarn that will knit to $3\frac{1}{2}$ stitches to the inch, on whatever size needle works for you. You'll be working on circular needles, in the round, from the bottom up. When you reach the arm area, you'll divide the piece in half. Half of the stitches you'll place on a stitch holder (this looks like a very big safety pin), and the other half you'll work as the back of the shirt. Both the back and front are worked the same, and you'll add a few stitches on each side for short sleeves. Finally, simple shoulder shaping will make your T-shirt fit just right.

This T-shirt is quick to knit and easy to wear. I've made several using different yarns, and the results are always reliable.

I've made this T using a wide variety of yarns, and it always comes out great. Be inspired by the fiber you choose! You may choose one of the many self-striping yarns available, or maybe a solid is more to your liking. Whatever yarn you choose, be sure you love the feel and will like it against your skin.

I've also included a shawl pattern later in this chapter as a partner for a great ensemble.

Finished size:

The sizing on this project is a bit different from what we've worked with so far, so let's talk about measurements and fit for a bit.

To determine your size, measure your chest circumference at the largest point. This number will guide you in the number of stitches you need, as well as the amount of yarn you need to buy. Because you'll be choosing your own yarn for this project, here is the yardage you'll need according to chest size based on a gauge of 3½ stitches per inch:

Extra small (36-inch chest circumference)	450 yards
Small (40 inches)	550 yards
Medium (44 inches)	650 yards
Large (48 inches)	700 yards
Extra large (52 inches)	800 yards

If you want to make the companion shawl, buy another 250 to 300 yards of yarn.

Be sure to check the label on your yarn. Balls and skeins are not equal. Some may have 82 yards, while another may have 250 yards. Be sure to buy enough for your whole project at one time. The dyes companies use vary, and you want to try to buy all your yarn from one dye lot to avoid differences in color. If the yarn you choose is variegated with a great amount of variation, the dye lot won't be as important.

In the pattern, the first number given refers to a small (36-inch) size. Numbers for 40-, 44-, 48-, and 52-inch circumference are listed in parentheses.

Materials:

Yarn of your choice. Be sure you have the correct yardage. The sample shown was knitted with Trendsetter Yarns' Treasure; 5 skeins, 155 yards per skein (100 grams); 45 percent wool, 38 percent polyester, 17 percent nylon.

The listed gauge on this yarn is 4 sts to 1 inch on a U.S. 10 needle. This yarn changes from a very thin fiber to a much thicker fiber, so the gauge isn't even throughout. Some of it measures 4 sts per inch while other sections measure 3½ sts per inch. That's a *big* difference! If you choose a yarn that changes from thick to thin, be sure your swatch is large enough so you can calculate the gauge in two or three places and then take an average. My average was 3½ sts per inch. The pattern is written according to this gauge.

Circular needle, probably 24 or 32 inches, depending on the number of stitches you need; I used a 24 inch

Stitch holder

2 stitch markers

Large-eye darning needle

Gauge:

3½ sts = 1 inch (The number of rows per inch may vary according to the yarn you choose. It's not important for this pattern. You'll be measuring the length as you go.)

Using the cable CO method, CO 116 (136, 156) sts.

Rnd 1: PM at beg of rnd, be sure all your sts are straight, and beg knitting in the round.

Rnd 2: P.

Rnd 3: K.

Rnd 4: P. (These first 4 rnds will give you a bottom edge that won't curl.)

Change to stockinette, and k all rnds until the piece measures 10 (11½, 13) inches.

Divide sts in half to work back and front in the same way.

Put half of sts 58 (68, 78) on st holder.

Work the back in stockinette, and beg inc rows from RS. You will be creating short sleeves.

Row 1: *K1, kf&b, k to end.

Row 2: K1, pf&b, p to end.

Rep Rows 1 and 2 two more times. You will have inc the number of sts by 6 (64 [74, 84 sts]).

Cable CO 13 sts at the beg of the next 2 rows (90 [100, 110 sts]).

Continue with stockinette until sleeve measures 7½ (8, 8½) inches. For a nice edge, sl the 1st st of all rows.

Shoulder shaping:

BO 8 (10, 12) sts at beg of next 4 rows.

BO 8 (9, 10) sts at beg of next 2 rows.

BO remaining 42 sts for neck.

Transfer sts from st holder onto the ndl, and rep from * to end.

Assembly:

With back and front RS in, place the BO edges next to each other and pin the shoulder edges together so the decreases meet up.

Sew the shoulder seam, working stitch by stitch.

Repeat the same technique for sewing up the sleeve seams.

Project: Dropped-Stitch Shawl

The sections on both ends of this shawl feature a dropped-stitch pattern, adding a lacing detail to the piece.

This dropped-stitch shawl can go dressy or casual.

When making this shawl, I used 2 skeins Trendsetter Treasure, knitting on U.S. 13 (9mm) needles. This made the fabric light and airy, a nice complement to the more densely knitted T-shirt.

Finished size:

20 inches W×56 inches L

Materials:

Approximately 200 yards yarn of your choice

U.S. 13 (9mm) straight or circular needles

Darning needle

Stitch pattern:

Dropped stitch:

Row 1: *K1, YO; rep to end.

Row 2: P.

CO 24 sts with practice yarn on size 10.5 ndls. Work garter st for 4 rows. Work dropped st for 2 rows, and rep garter st for 4 rows. Cont until piece measures 6 inches. BO.

Using the same yarn as your T, CO 50 sts.

*Work garter st for 4 rows.

Work dropped st for 2 rows.

Rep from * two more times.

Work garter st until piece measures 55 inches from CO.

Alternate dropped st rows with 4 rows of garter st three times.

BO.

The Least You Need to Know

- Gauge depends on the yarn you choose, the needle size, and the way you knit. Always make a swatch before starting your project.
- Measuring your gauge is critical to the successful creation of a garment.
- When you purchase yarn, buy enough for your whole garment plus an additional skein, hank, or ball. You want to be sure all the yarn comes from the same dye lot if possible. This guarantees consistent color throughout your garment.

More Shaping Techniques

In This Chapter

- Creating strong, smooth seams
- Learning the three-needle bind-off
- Picking up stitches to create edges and collars

Smooth, even seams are the mark of good craftsmanship. You'll be so much more comfortable wearing your hand-knitted garments knowing that the seams are secure and well done. For shoulder seams, one of the best ways of ensuring a great look is using the three-needle bind-off. This is one of two finishing techniques we explore in this chapter.

You can add collars, pockets, and edgings by picking up stitches along edges. You'll use this technique in many situations. In this chapter, we add a decorative edging along the front of a vest.

The Three-Needle Bind-Off

Making accurate and professional-looking seams is a cinch with the three-needle bind-off. This technique is particularly useful for shoulder seams. The idea is to bind off two edges while at the same time knitting them together. This creates a perfectly even seam.

Swatch It!

For this swatch, you need two sets of needles that are the same size. If you don't have two sets of the same size, use a second set that's one size smaller or larger than the other.

Make 2 swatches with your practice yarn by CO 15 sts for each and working garter stitch for 2 rows and stockinette for 10 rows. Do not BO either swatch.

For the first swatch, leave the sts on the ndl and cut the yarn, leaving a 6-inch tail. Do not cut the working yarn on the 2nd swatch.

Hold the ndls with the sts together in your left hand, parallel to each other, with RS (knit sides) facing you. The ndl with the working yarn should be farthest from you.

Insert a 3rd ndl into the 1st sts on both ndls knitwise (to the left of the 1st st). Put it through the st on the ndl closest to you and then through the st on the ndl behind it.

Wrap the yarn around the point, and k the 2 sts at the same time.

Bring the yarn back through both sts.

Slide off both of the old sts, leaving 1 st on the right ndl.

Rep for the next st. You should now have 2 sts on the right ndl.

Pass the 1st st on the right ndl over the 2nd one, just as you would in a regular BO.

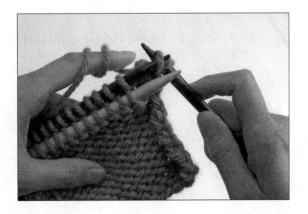

Cont until all the sts are BO and you have 1 stitch left on the right ndl. The 2 swatches will be linked together.

Cut the working yarn, leaving a 6-inch tail, and pull it through the last st.

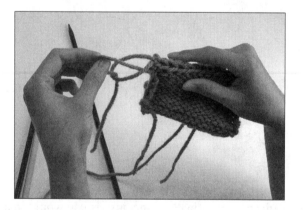

You will have 2 tails to weave into your fabric—one from the BO and the other from the 2nd swatch.

Take a good look at your seam. It should be even, and the right side should be very smooth.

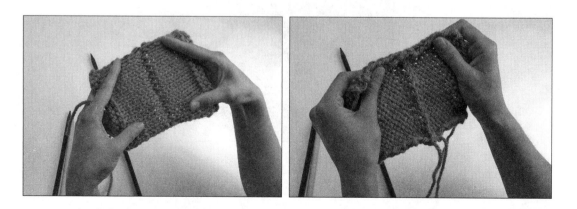

Picking Up Stitches on a Bind-Off Edge

In many situations, you'll need to pick up stitches. You may be creating a collar, a pocket, a sleeve, edging, or a whole section of a garment. Once you pick up the stitches, you can knit the section without having to sew it on later.

Swatch It!

CO 15 sts, and k a garter st swatch 20 rows long. BO.

Choose a contrasting color yarn and a slightly smaller needle. Starting at the top-right corner of your swatch, work across the BO row. The working yarn should be behind the swatch.

Insert the ndl into the 1st V from the front to the back.

Leaving a 6-inch tail in the back, wrap the yarn around the tip of the ndl knitwise.

Pull the loop through toward you, and leave it on the ndl.

Rep preceding steps three more times. After a few sts, give the tail a gentle tug to keep it in place.

 UNRAVELING

At first, you might find it difficult to maneuver the needle, and sometimes the yarn will slide off as you try to pick up the new stitches. Use your right index finger to help keep the yarn at the tip of your needle as you pull it through to the front.

I find it easier to pick up the stitches using a crochet hook. With this method, you don't have to use a smaller needle. You can use the same size needle specified for knitting the section.

Insert the hook from the front to the back, the same as using the ndl.

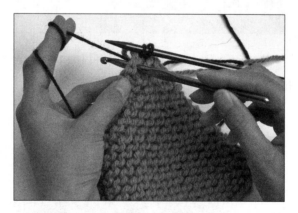

Loop the st on the hook, and pull through.

Smart, fashionable, and easy to complete in a weekend, this little black bag can be embellished to show your sophistication—or your sense of humor! (Chapter 10)

A simple bouquet of knitted flowers makes this pillow a standout on any sofa or easy chair. (Chapter 19)

A great pair of first projects, you can knit this hat and scarf in many sizes, from children to adult. (Chapters 2 and 3)

Hand-dyed yarn creates lovely random patterns in this vest. (Chapter 13)

Create your own stripes when you change yarns and colors in this warm beret. (Chapter 11) ▶

Easy to knit and easy to wear, this T-shirt and shawl complement anything from a skirt to jeans. (Chapter 12)

A felted tote is a sturdy companion, great for carrying everything from groceries to a laptop. (Chapter 21)

This fun jacket is a wonderful cover-up ▶ when the weather turns chilly. (Chapter 18)

Wrapped in this fortune cookie hooded ▶
blanket, your little bundle of love will
stay snug and warm. (Chapter 9)

◀ You'll find it hard to resist
curling up on this soft, comfy
knitted rug. (Chapter 16)

Luxurious and warm, this stole
can be worn alone or over a coat.
(Chapter 15)

Knit him something to keep him
warm and cozy. (Chapter 17)

Join the sock craze! This small project is perfect to knit as you travel. (Chapter 14)

Building blocks of color and shapes make entrelac projects fun to knit. (Chapter 20)

Enlarging the squares of the knitted sampler you create using the 15 stitch patterns you learn throughout the book produces an eye-catching afghan. (Chapter 8)

Place the loop on the ndl.

Finish the row in the same manner.

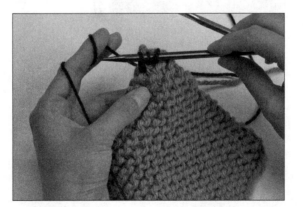

Picking Up Stitches Around a Vertical Edge

When you pick up stitches along a cast-on or bind-off edge, you can easily see each stitch. Picking up stitches along the vertical edge is a little trickier because the vertical edge shows you each row as opposed to each stitch.

You may remember that when you calculate gauge, stitches per inch and rows per inch aren't exactly the same measurement. There are usually more rows per inch. Consequently, you have to improvise a little to get the best look. Sometimes that means adding an additional stitch every so often so your pick-up stitches are even and lay flat.

1. Position the swatch so the side edge or vertical edge is at the top.

2. Insert the ndl or crochet hook between the 1st 2 rows.

3. Wrap the yarn around the ndl, and pull it through.

4. Rep steps 1 through 3 to finish.

Now you're ready to begin knitting the edge or collar. When you have the number of rows you need, be sure you bind off carefully to avoid too-tight or too-loose stitches. You want your finishing to add flair and great panache to your piece.

Project: Diamond Lace Vest

This kimono-style vest is comfortable, dressy, and perfect for wear nearly any time of the year. The yarn is so yummy and feels so good in your hands, you almost won't want the knitting to end!

The yarn used in this pattern is just yummy! Working with it was a joy because of the combination of silk, wool, and mohair.

Because the vest is loose-fitting, the pattern can be made in two sizes: small/medium and large/extra large. It's made in one piece, knitting back and forth on long circular needles, up to the decreases for the armholes. Then you divide the stitches for the back, right front, and left front. You work the back next, followed by each front panel. You use the three-needle bind-off technique for perfect shoulder seams. Finally, you pick up stitches for a collar band that will finish the piece in style.

Finished size:

40 (44) inches chest; 21 (22) inches length

Materials:

10 (11) skeins Fiesta Yarns, Flurry; 47 percent silk, 35 percent wool, 18 percent mohair; 110 yards per skein; 2 ounces (57 grams); Sandstone

U.S. 10 (6mm) 24- or 32-inch circular needles for body (Adjust needle size to obtain the correct gauge.)

U.S. 10 (6mm) straight needles

U.S. 11 (8mm) 24- or 32-inch circular needle for collar band

Large-eye darning needle

U.S. I crochet hook (optional for picking up stitches)

3 stitch holders

Gauge:

4 sts = 1 inch; 5 rows = 1 inch

Stitch pattern:

Diagonal cluster lace:

Row 1: (WS) P.

Row 2: K2, *YO, k3, pass 1st of the 3 knit sts over the 2nd and 3rd sts; rep from * to end, k1. (Do not YO before the last st. If you do, you will be adding a st.)

Row 3: P.

Row 4: K1, *k3, pass 1st of the 3 knit sts over the 2nd and 3rd sts, YO; rep from * to end k2. (Remember to YO before the last 2 sts in this row.)

JAZZING IT UP

Remembering a few hints while working will make this project go smoother: don't forget your YOs, and be careful not to pull them tight. And take your measurements on a flat surface. In addition to measuring, count your rows to be sure the back and the fronts are the same lengths. Finally, working with the large number of stitches at the beginning may be more comfortable with a circular needle, even though you're knitting back and forth. Once you begin working with the smaller sections, a straight needle may be preferable.

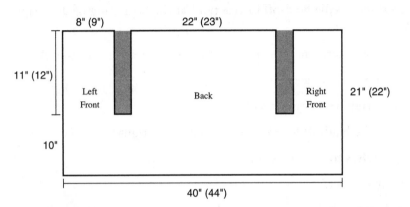

The schematic shows the measurements for the two sizes. The small size is first, followed by the larger size in parentheses.

Working up from the bottom edge:

Using the long-tail cast-on, CO 162 (177) sts. This CO requires about 4 yards (4.5 yards) of tail.

Work the diagonal cluster lace st patt until the piece measures 10 inches from CO row. End with RS facing you.

Decrease for armholes and work back:

Cont with st patt for 35 (37) sts; BO next 4 sts.

Place 1st 35 (37) sts on st holder.

Cont in st patt to end of row.

P 35 (37) sts; BO next 4 sts.

Place 1st 35 (37) sts on st holder, and continue working back section.

When back section measures 20 (21) inches from CO edge, put all back section sts on st holder.

Work right front:

Transfer sts of right front section from st holder to your ndl.

Cont working in st patt until the piece measures 20 (21) inches from CO edge. Place sts back on st holder.

Work left front:

Rep same instructions as right front.

Three-needle bind-off:

Transfer sts of back section onto straight ndl.

Position RS of back section against RS of left front, and line up the sts. Be sure the points of the ndls are in the same direction. If they're not, transfer one or the other onto another ndl. (See the three-needle bind-off instructions at the beginning of the chapter if you need a refresher.)

BO 35 (37) sts using three-needle bind-off method to attach front to back.

BO 18 (21) sts for back of neck.

Transfer sts for right front onto needle.

Work three-needle bind-off for 35 (37) sts, combining right front to remaining back sts.

Picking up stitches for collar band:

Turn vest right side out.

Using the U.S. 11 circ ndl, begin at CO edge of right front section, and pick up sts along the vertical edge, around the neck, and back down the edge of the left front.

P the next row, working your way back up the left front, around the neck, and down the right front.

K the next row, and continue with stockinette st for 12 more rows. BO. The collar band should curl toward the outside of the garment, creating a soft edged finish.

Weave in all loose ends, and enjoy!

The Least You Need to Know

- Three-needle bind-off creates smooth, even, and very professional-looking seams.
- Picking up stitches along edges enables you to add collars, pockets, and edges to your work.
- Always measure your "work in progress" on a flat surface. This is the best way to get accurate measurements.

Sock Construction

In This Chapter

- The joy of knitting socks
- Figuring out sizes
- Tools for knitting socks
- Working the kitchener stitch

Years ago, knitting socks was a necessity in every household. In Colonial days, American knitters coveted yarn, both locally spun and imported, for the socks they needed to make for their families. Knitting groups formed to knit socks to support soldiers during the Revolutionary and Civil Wars.

Now sock knitting is a creative endeavor. I know some knitters who always have a pair or two in process. I see them walking around yarn shows as they knit, a little bag dangling from their wrist containing the yarn and needles clicking in their hands.

Sock Construction Zone

Socks are a popular item to knit. Some of the inspiration has been generated by the variety of sock yarns. You can buy hand-dyed yarns and others that are dyed in such a way that they create complex patterns just in the knitting. Fiber content is varied and so are the weights, from superfine fingering yarn you knit on size 0 or 1 needles to thicker yarns comfortably knit on size 7s. And Converse and other shoe manufacturers are now making transparent shoes that really let your handiwork shine through!

There's a simple formula for calculating the size of a sock:

> 100 percent of the stitches are worked for the leg.
>
> 50 percent for the heel.
>
> 100 percent for the foot.
>
> You decrease for the toe to 50 percent and then down to 20 percent.

You calculate the number of stitches according to the gauge of the yarn you're using.

Many patterns begin with the leg and work down to the toe, while others begin with the toe and reverse the process. Rib stitch patterns are used at the cuff to prevent curling. Many other stitch patterns can be incorporated in the leg and foot areas, as you like.

A simple approach begins with the leg and works down to the heel flap, where the stitches divide for the heel and foot. You then knit the heel flap and work a *gusset*, which enables you to connect the heel with the instep and work in the round all the way to the toe area.

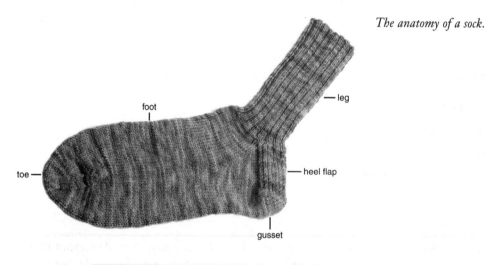

The anatomy of a sock.

DEFINITION

The **gusset** of a sock is a knitted piece that connects the stitches from the leg section to the stitches of the heel flap. To create the gusset, you pick up stitches along the leg section, gradually decreasing them to the point where you have the original number of stitches and are working the foot section.

Sock-Knitting Needle Options

You can knit socks at different gauges on needle sizes ranging from U.S. 1 to U.S. 11 and with yarn from superfine to bulky.

You can use four double-pointed needles, five double-pointed needles, a 12-inch circular needle, two circular needles, or a very long circular needle (40 inches long) with a method called the magic loop, which we explore in a moment.

The Kitchener Stitch

The kitchener stitch is used for seaming and for the toe area on socks. When you've finished the toe using this technique, it looks invisible. Like the three-needle bind-off, you need the same number of stitches on two needles. Unlike the three-needle bind-off, you use a tapestry needle to sew the seam together.

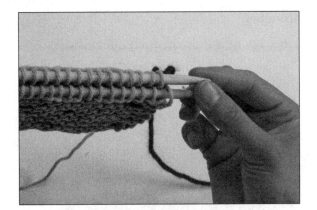

There are two set-up steps and four repeating steps to the kitchener stitch:

Set-up steps—do each one once:

1. With the working yarn coming from the back ndl, insert the tapestry ndl through the first st from right to left (purlwise) on the front ndl.

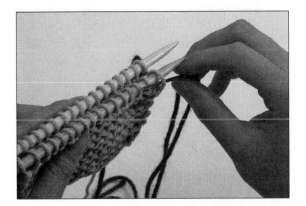

2. Insert ndl through 1st st on the back ndl from left to right (knitwise).

Repeating steps 1 through 4:

1. Insert the ndl through next st on the front ndl knitwise.

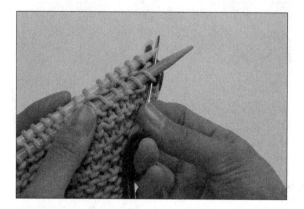

2. Sl the first sts on front ndl off.

3. Insert the ndl purlwise through next st on the front ndl. *Do not slip it off.*

4. Insert the ndl purlwise into the 1st st on the back ndl.

5. Sl off.

6. Insert the ndl knitwise into next st on the back ndl. *Do not slip it off.*

7. Rep steps 1 through 4 until all sts are sewn together.

A STITCH IN TIME

Portland, Oregon, hosted the first Sock Summit in 2009, drawing dozens of teachers and thousands of knitters from all over North America. The event featured the Sock Museum, tracing the history of socks and the various materials and patterns used back to the Roman period. For more information, visit socksummit.com.

Project: Comfy Socks

This pair of socks is made using the magic loop method of knitting in the round. It's less cumbersome than using double-pointed needles, and you'll have less of a problem with loose stitches where you transfer from one needle to the next.

Beginning at the top of the sock, the cuff and leg are knit in the round, and the heel flap and heel turn are knit in rows on half of the stitches. Next, stitches are picked up around the heel flap, and knitting continues in the round for the gusset shaping, foot, and toe.

A sock project is a very portable one, and it's great to take on trips. All you need are your needles, a pattern, and one skein or ball of yarn.

Finished size:

Fits a woman's foot up to U.S. 8.5

Materials:

1 skein Dream in Color Smooshy sock yarn; 100 percent superfine Australian Merino superwash; 450 yards; 4 ounces (113 grams); Beach Fog

U.S. 2 (2.75mm) 40-inch circular needle

2 stitch markers

Gauge:

8 sts = 1 inch; 10 rows = 1 inch

Abbreviations:

sl st	slip stitch
SM	slip marker
wyib	with yarn in back
wyif	with yarn in front

Leg:

Using the long-tail cast-on, CO 64 sts.

Put sts on the cable part of the ndl.

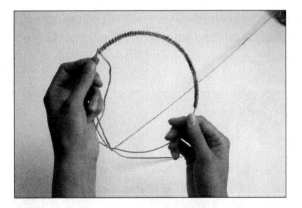

Divide the sts in half by locating where the 32nd and 33rd sts are, and fold and pull the cable part of the ndl at this point.

Slide each group of 32 sts toward the points of the ndl. Be sure the sts aren't twisted.

Note: From here on, to label to the points of the needle, I refer to the "front" needle and the "back" needle. The working yarn should be coming from the back needle.

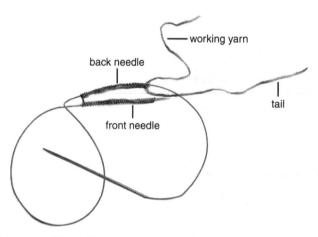

Beg the 1st rnd of knitting by pulling on the back ndl so the sts on that ndl slide onto the cable, and you've pulled out enough cable so you can use the tip of the back ndl to work the sts on the front ndl.

Work in k2, p2 rib across the 32 sts of the front ndl.

JAZZING IT UP

If you prefer not to knit the entire leg in k2, p2 rib, work in rib for 1 inch and then work rest of leg in stockinette. When knitting in the round, you'd be knitting all stitches every round.

Turn your work around, making the ndl with the sts on it the back ndl.

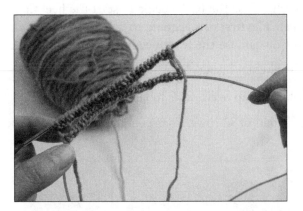

Pull on the cable until the sts that were on the cable come to the point of the ndl that's now the front ndl. Rep the process of pulling out the back ndl and working across the sts on the front ndl in k2, p2 rib. That's 1 rnd completed.

Note: Until your knitting has been established for a few rounds, your needles might want to "roll" a bit, making it seem like the front and back needles are exchanging places. Don't worry much about this. Before continuing, roll them back into the proper position, so the working yarn is always coming from the back needle.

Cont in this manner in k2, p2 rib until the piece measures 7 inches or desired length of cuff and leg.

> **UNRAVELING**
>
> I enjoy using the magic loop and find it works well for sock knitting. Just be careful when you pull on the cable when changing rows. I once pulled too hard, and all the stitches came off the needle! I spent 20 minutes with a small crochet hook putting the stitches back in place on the needle. Whew!

Heel flap:

The heel flap is made using half of the stitches. You work back and forth in rows, the same number of rows as stitches. Use the back needle to start the heel flap (the yarn is already attached to this needle). The first row is going to be on the WS. Slide the stitches on the front needle to the cable so you can use the front needle for working the heel flap.

Row 1: K1, purl to the last st, sl 1, wyif.

Row 2: K1, *sl 1, wyib, k1* (rep between *s to last st), sl 1 wyif.

Rep these 2 rows for a total of 32 rows. Your heel flap is now complete.

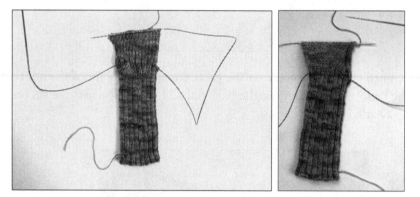

This is the heel flap seen from the right side (left) and the wrong side (right).

Heel turn:

Continuing with the stitches from the heel flap, you'll also work in short or partial rows for the heel turn, beginning on the wrong side:

Row 1: Sl 1, p16, p2tog, p1, turn work. *Note:* This will create gaps between sts.

Row 2: Sl 1, k3, ssk, k1, turn.

Row 3: Sl 1, purl to within 1 st of the gap between the sts and p2tog (the sts on each side of the gap), p1, turn.

Row 4: Sl 1, k to within 1 st of the gap and ssk, k1, turn.

Rep Rows 3 and 4 five more times.

You should have 18 sts remaining on 1 ndl and the instep sts on the other ndl.

With RS facing, pick up and k 16 sts in the selvedge sts from the side of the heel flap, and pick up and k 2 more sts from the end of the heel flap to the next ndl to close that gap. PM.

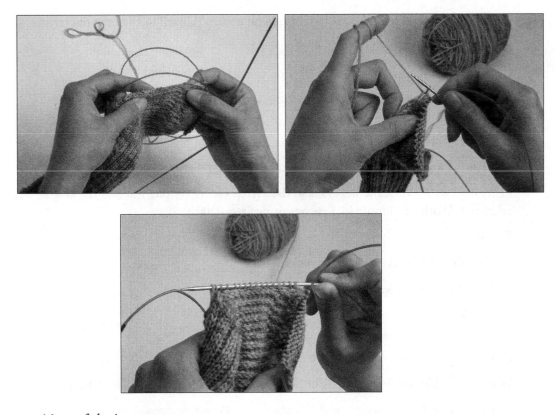

K across 16 sts of the instep.

Begin magic loop knitting again, and for the 2nd ndl, work across the remaining 16 sts of the instep, PM, pick up and k2 to close the gap.

Then pick up and k16 in the selvedge sts along the side of the heel flap, and finish with 9 sts from the back of the heel.

Each ndl has 43 sts and is holding half the sock. Work 1 rnd.

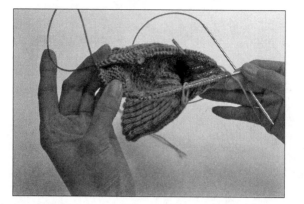

To be sure you're in the right place, think of the sock laying flat, like a figure-8. Half of the sts from the middle of the heel to the middle of the instep are on one ndl and the other half on the other ndl.

Begin gusset decrease until you have 32 sts on each ndl, back to the original 64 sts.

Rnd 1: dec rnd:

> Ndl 1: K to 3 sts before marker, k2tog, k1, SM, k to end of ndl.
>
> Ndl 2: K to marker, SM, k1, k2tog, k to end of ndl.

Rnd 2: K all sts on both ndls, SM.

Rep Rnds 1 and 2 until you have 32 sts on each ndl, 64 sts total.

Rearrange sts as you k the next rnd so the instep sts are on one ndl and the sole sts are on the other ndl. Work until foot is 7.5 inches or desired length.

Toe shaping:

The toe decs are worked the same way on each ndl:

> Rnd 1: K1, ssk, k to last 3 sts, k2tog, k1.
>
> Rnd 2: K all sts.

Rep Rnds 1 and 2 until you have 16 sts on each ndl, 32 sts total.

Work Rnd 1 (do not work Rnd 2) until you have 8 sts on each ndl, 16 sts total.

Graft together the toe sts using the kitchener st. Weave in ends.

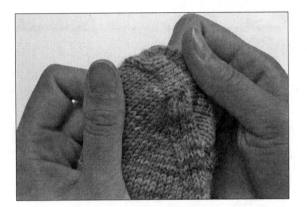

Rep for 2nd sock.

The Least You Need to Know

- Socks are knitted in the round on tiny circulars, double-pointed needles, or on a long circular called a magic loop.
- You can knit socks from the top of the cuff down to the toes or the reverse.
- The kitchener stitch is a finishing technique for seamlessly joining two edges and is commonly used to finish the seam at the toe of a sock.

Using Big Needles and Bulky Yarn

In This Chapter

- Big needles and how to use them comfortably
- Fun with bulky yarns
- Needle felting for a perfect finish

In Chapter 14, we worked on size 2 needles. In this chapter, we kick things up a few notches—and a few sizes!—by working with large needles. Working big makes the knitting go very fast. For those who love instant gratification, this is the way to go.

Big needles are available in plastic and wood but not metal. The metal needles would likely be too heavy to handle, so lightweight materials are much preferred when working at this scale. Circulars are available, but I prefer the straight needles because it can be difficult to work your stitches up from the cable or tubing onto the needle part of the circulars. My favorites are the straight needles. You can knit with them in your lap while sitting on a couch or on the floor.

Working with Big Needles

I love working with big needles. And when I say "big needles," I mean BIG needles—the largest available, sizes U.S. 35 (19mm) and 50 (25mm)! When you use these large needles, your pieces work up very quickly.

Using large needles is very easy on your eyes and your hands. If you're working with size 50 needles, your gauge is approximately 1 stitch per 1 inch! And because the stitches are so large, you don't need to hold your work close to your eyes to see them. With the monster needles, you'll find it's easier to relax and rather than holding up your work, you can knit with the needles in your lap—and not even hold them tightly.

When working with the big needles, use the long-tail cast-on, and cast on loosely. The first row is always a little stiff to work, just like smaller needles. Figure about 2.5 inches per stitch with the size 50 needles.

A STITCH IN TIME

Some people are more comfortable using the English method with the big needles, so that's what I've modeled in this chapter's photos.

Here are some suggestions for getting comfortable with the big sticks:

- Hold the needles in your lap.

- Work the stitches at the points of the needles. Because your lap is holding the weight, you don't need much wrist movement.

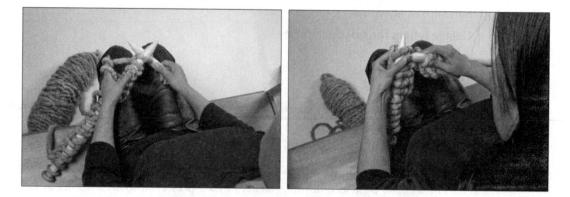

What can you make with these behemoth needles? Scarves, shawls, blankets, rugs, and pillows are just a few ideas, but really, the possibilities are endless!

Fun with Bulky Yarns

You wouldn't want to use a single strand of regular, worsted weight yarn with the large needles. Instead, match size for size and opt for bulky yarns.

Yarn standard 5 is called "bulky," and yarn standard 6 is called "super bulky." The latter includes very thick yarns and *roving* and *top*. You can find these and other bulky yarns from a wide range of sources.

Many manufacturers make bulky or super-bulky yarn. You can even work with roving on the super-big needles.

DEFINITION

Before natural fiber is spun into yarn, it goes through several processes. It's sorted according to length and grade of fiber. Then it's washed and combed. **Roving** is a long piece, about 2 to 4 inches in diameter, with the fiber laying in random directions. It's not combed. **Top** is a long piece like roving, sometimes referred to as *worsted top*. Unlike roving, top is prepared by combing, which keeps the wool fibers parallel to each other. The result is what looks like a very long, thick, snakelike yarn. Neither roving nor top are spun.

You can "make" your own yarns by combining a variety of weights. If you have yarn left over from projects or single skeins and balls in your stash, you can sort them by color and weight. Then combine them in groups of six or more fibers, depending on their thickness, and begin knitting. Try a few swatches, and see if you like your combinations. (I cover working with multiple fibers together in Chapter 16.)

> **A STITCH IN TIME**
>
> For many years, British fiber artist Rachel John has promoted working with big needles. She calls her work *extreme knitting*. In 2006, Rachel took extreme knitting to a new level she calls *monumental knitting*. At a UK fiber festival called Unravel, Rachel combined 1,000 strands of fiber simultaneously and knitted on gigantic needles. The result of this hand-knit masterpiece was a mattress. You can watch Rachel's achievement on YouTube: www.youtube.com/watch?v=VVRfVEONxJQ.

Needle Felting Finishing

The finishing for our practice piece, the Cable and Rib Stole, requires needle felting. This is due to the thickness of the yarn—it won't weave in behind other stitches because it's so large. So for this project, the tails need to be felted into the piece so they won't pop out.

Needle felting is quite simple. The process involves using a needle or multiple-needle tool and repeatedly poking it to work the fibers into each other. If you look at natural fibers through a microscope, you'll see they're covered with scales. When you work the needle felting tool into the layers of fiber, the scales hook on to each other, forming a tight bond.

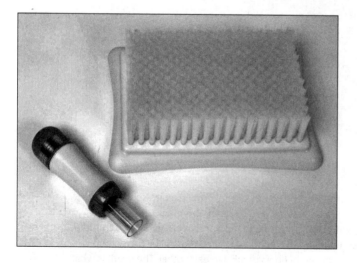

Needle felting tools include the needle tool and the mat. You can also use individual needles, but be careful—they're extremely sharp!

When you needle felt, you poke the fibers into each other so the scales on one fiber stick to the ones next to it.

You'll find many other opportunities for needle felting projects. It's a wonderful technique for adding embellishments to sweaters, pillows, jackets, and shawls.

Project: Cable and Rib Stole

In Chapter 7, we explored the cable and rib pattern on size 10.5 needles. Now we're going to use that same pattern on size 50 needles when making this stole.

This stole works up in just a few hours and is a great fall accessory. The pattern is a 4-row repeat.

Finished size:

22 inches W×54 inches L

Materials:

> 1 bump BagSmith's Big Stitch Alpaca Yarn; 70 percent alpaca, 15 percent wool, 15 percent nylon; 140 yards; 33 ounces (935 grams); color of your choice

> U.S. 50 (25mm) 20-inch straight needles

> Large double-pointed needle, cable needle, or large pen

> Needle felting tool and brush or foam pad

Gauge:

> 3 sts = 4 inches; 4.5 rows = 4 inches

Abbreviations:

> cn   cable needle

CO 18 sts.

Row 1: (RS) P3, k2, p2, k4, p2, k2, p3.

Row 2: P5, k2, p4, k2, p5.

Row 3: P3, k2, p2, sl 2 sts to double point or cn and hold in front, k next 2 sts on left ndl, k2 from cn, p2, k2, p3.

Row 4: Rep Row 2.

Rep 4-row st patt until you have just enough yarn to k about 1 more row. BO. Cut the tails so they're about 3 or 4 inches long, and needle felt them into the fabric.

The Least You Need to Know

- Bulky yarns and multiple yarns work best on big needles.
- Projects work up quickly on big needles.
- Needle felting is a process where the scales on individual strands of fiber are forced together, making them bind securely.

Knitting with Multiple Yarns

In This Chapter

- Effective ways of combining yarns
- Don't let the worms get you down
- The fun of working with your stash

As you become more involved with the fiber arts, your collection of yarn is sure to grow. It will probably be made up of yarns you see in shops that you just know you'll work into a project at some point, along with bits and pieces left over from projects you complete. This stash of yarn can become a great source of inspiration and creativity.

Think of it as an artist thinks of tubes of color or a composer thinks of the wide variety of sounds available in an orchestra. You don't necessarily use every color or sound in every piece. You choose combinations carefully and with purpose. So it is with the fiber in your stash.

Yarns That Play Well Together

If you've worked along with each chapter in the book so far, you've probably started accumulating a bunch of leftover yarn. You may also be stockpiling a stash of yarns for undetermined future projects.

In my many years of attending shows and meeting knitters, I can only remember one person who told me she doesn't have a stash; others have admitted to drawers and closets full of yarns of all descriptions. I'll never forget a knitter who frequented our BagSmith booth at STITCHES East, one of four annual yarn and fiber shows sponsored by *Knitter's Magazine*. She came back 3 days in a row to purchase various kinds of yarns and supplies. In a discussion about one of the yarns, she told me her husband always goes on a fishing trip the weekend she attends this show, and thankfully, all her purchases would be neatly squirreled away before his return.

Whether or not you have a growing stash or you just want to buy yarns that will work well together, by following some guidelines, you'll set yourself up for successful fiber combining.

Begin by organizing your yarns according to color group. Shoot for roughly eight groups, including white, yellow, green, red, blue, purple, brown, and black.

Some yarns may be variegated and may span a few groups. Others will be a close call and may fit in more than one group. Don't obsess over it; just put them where they fit the best.

Chenille and acrylic mohair do not play well with others. Keep these fibers away from groups.

Combining thick and thin fibers is fine. Just watch out for the thin ones that tend to curl. These will eventually *worm* in your knitting.

> **DEFINITION**
>
> **Worming** can occur with many different yarns but is very common with chenille. You will be knitting along happily and look down and suddenly see extra yarn poking out of place in a curly fashion. This is your worm. If you're working with multiple fibers and see a worm, you can knot it, cut it off close to the knot, and hide the knot in the other fibers. If you're working with just the one fiber, it's best to go back to the worm itself, straighten it out, and begin knitting again.

The greater number of yarns you combine and the thicker the fibers, the more dense your stitches will be.

Always swatch the fibers you choose to work with on your project. This helps you test for worming, see how the colors combine, and measure your gauge.

To maintain a consistent gauge, be sure that when you run out of a fiber, replace it with the same fiber or one of a similar weight.

When joining two ends (new yarn to the working yarn), use an overhand knot to tie the ends together, leaving a short tail.

If you are only using two or three fibers, leave longer tails when joining ends. You can weave or crochet in the ends for a more finished look.

To ensure all the fibers are caught in each stitch, slide your left thumb under all the fibers.

Keeping Yarns in Their Proper Place

When you're working with multiple yarns, you'll quickly learn that the yarns can easily tangle if you're not careful. To minimize this, it helps if you place your yarns in containers before you begin working.

Managing your yarn is important when you work with multiple fibers. Some knitters use mixing bowls to keep their yarns separate; others use cardboard boxes, plastic bags, or shoe boxes. Use whatever works best for you.

You can comfortably put four balls in a container. If you're using cones, put them close together so they won't fall over and roll around.

As you knit with multiple yarns, smooth out the strands as you pull them up from the container. You can work out any knots that way and be sure any problems are addressed before they reach your needles.

Project: Spiral Rug

This spiral rug project gives you an opportunity to use your stash if you don't want to use the specified yarns. If you want to use thinner yarns, combine 6 or 7 together and knit a swatch to see if you like the combination.

You can create a beautiful area rug in a short time using this pattern.

This kind of project is a great opportunity to experiment with different yarns, textures, and colors. The spiral rug works up very quickly, and you can have a new look to your favorite room in just a few hours.

Finished size:

Approximately 36 inches in diameter

Materials:

2 (16-ounce; 453-gram) BagSmith Big Stitch Bundles; each with 12 yarns, including wool, wool blends, and acrylic; each yarn is 40 yards; total yardage for the bundle is 480 yards

U.S. 35 (19mm) needles

Darning needle

Gauge:

Not critical

Stitch pattern:

Garter stitch: K every row.

Abbreviations:

skp   slip, knit, pass slipped stitch over knit stitch

JAZZING IT UP

This rug is knit in very short rows, and you turn your work often. If you turn your work in continuous circles, the long, snakelike piece you're making will twist. If you transfer the needle with the stitches back and forth, you reduce the amount of twisting and time it takes to put the swirl in place. This makes it easier for you to lay out the piece after knitting. Ultimately, the curl is not permanent, so either way you want to do it is fine.

Note: Before beginning, carefully take apart the Big Bundle, rolling up each individual yarn separately. Use 6 of the fibers simultaneously, and change them as you like as you go.

With 6 fibers, CO 1 st and k 8 rows.

Kf&b (2 sts).

K all sts for next 12 rows.

K1, m1, k1 (3 sts).

K for next 52 rows.

K1, m1, k2 (4 sts).

K for next 94 rows.

K1, m1, k3 (5 sts).

K for next 150 rows. With some contrasting yarn, mark every 25 rows to keep track of where you are.

Begin decrease rows:

K1, skp (4 sts).

K for 20 rows.

K1, skp, k1 (3 sts).

K for 16 rows.

K1, skp (2 sts).

K for 12 rows.

K2tog and k single st for 8 rows.

BO st.

Assembly:

On a table, floor, or another flat surface, place the knitted piece wrong side up in the swirl pattern, making sure all sides are completely flat. You'll be sewing it together on the back side of the piece.

Using one of the thick yarns, begin sewing the sides together from the outside toward the inside. Continue around the swirl, working your stitches carefully so they're secure but not pulled too tight.

Weave in the ends, turn right side up, and place in a special place!

Want to make a larger rug? When you get to the 5-stitch increase (step 9), knit more rows before you begin the decrease section. To increase the diameter, continue knitting the 5 stitches until you have enough length to make another complete circle around the spiral.

The Least You Need to Know

- Remember that not all yarns will play well together, and be careful when combining fibers. Chenille is a big culprit and will worm frequently.
- Organize your yarn so the fibers don't have a chance to tangle. Use boxes, bowls, bags, or other containers to corral your yarns.
- Always swatch your combinations. Be sure they work well together before you start stitching your project.

Adapting Sizes

In This Chapter

- Working on great-fitting garments
- Measuring accurately
- Shaping sleeves and collars

Ask any knitter, and he or she will have a horror story or two to tell about garments they made that didn't fit. The finished pieces go into the trash, the charity box, a back corner of a closet, or in a to-frog pile. (Frogging is the process of ripping out your work—rip it, rip it! See more about this in Chapter 24.) The frustration can be enormous, especially after the excitement of creating a garment and all the time and hours spent knitting. But it doesn't have to be that way.

In this chapter, I walk you through perhaps the most important part of knitting clothing: measuring. You'll be amazed how successful you'll be if you follow a few simple tips.

Measure Twice, Knit Once

You can check and double-check gauge. You can follow a pattern exactly. But your finished sweater is far from the correct size or shape for you. This is a common problem, but by following a few rules before you start and while you work, you can avoid disappointment later:

- Take measurements accurately. The more exact your measurements, the easier it will be to choose the correct size to make.

- Check your gauge carefully, and be sure it matches the requirements of the pattern. If it doesn't, change your needle size until you have the correct gauge (or change the yarn).

- Take your time, and measure again. The old builder's advice "measure twice, cut once" applies to knitting as well.

For a relaxed-style sweater without much tailoring, you need four measurements:

- Chest circumference
- Length
- Sleeve length
- Collar

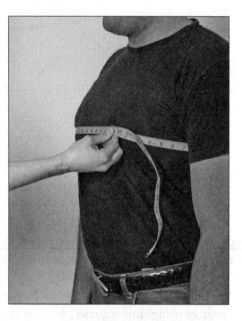

To get an accurate chest measurement, measure around the fullest part of the bust/chest.

When measuring for length, measure from the top of the shoulder to the hip.

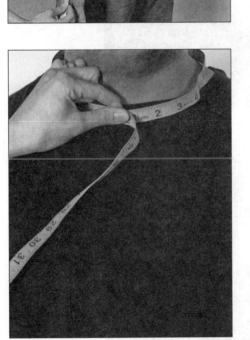

To determine sleeve length, measure from the top of the shoulder to the wrist.

Measure from the back of the neck around to the front and back again to get the collar measurement.

With these four measurements in hand, you're well on your way to making a nice-fitting sweater.

Picking Up Stitches for Sleeves and Collar

Some patterns are designed so the sleeves are separate pieces you must sew on later. Others have you pick up the stitches along the side edges and knit the sleeves down to the wrist. The practice project in this chapter uses the latter technique. You pick up stitches for the sleeves after you've sewn together the shoulders. You pick up half of the stitches on one side of the shoulder seam, and then pick up the other half on the other side of the shoulder seam. The right side should be facing you.

Here's how it works:

1. With RS facing you, place 1 pin at the shoulder seam and another 11 inches to the left of the seam.

2. Rep on RS.

3. Beg at the left pin, pick up sts between every row along the selvedge edge.

One stitch is picked up and on the needle.

Here you've picked up 3 stitches.

Now you have all the stitches you need for the sleeve on your needle.

To be sure the sleeves are the correct length, you can try on the piece and evaluate the sleeve length before you bind it off.

Project: Boyfriend's Sweater

This man's drop-shoulder sweater is loose and comfortable, and the yarn is a cozy, bulky wool.

From a college classroom to a fall football game, this sweater is sure to become an old friend.

The sweater is knit in the mock rib stitch pattern. The back and front are knit from the bottom up and joined at the shoulders using the three-needle bind-off. After connecting the shoulders, you pick up the sleeve stitches from the body of the sweater and knit down to the cuff. Around the collar, you pick up stitches around the neck and knit the collar in the round.

Finished size:

44 (48, 52) inches

Materials:

9 (10, 11) skeins Berroco Peruvia Quick; 100 percent Peruvian Highland Wool; 103 yards per skein; 3.5 ounces (100 grams)

2 U.S. 10.5 straight or circular needles

U.S. 10.5 16-inch circular needle

2 U.S. 11 needles; at least 1 needs to be a 24-inch circular

3 stitch holders

Stitch marker

Gauge:

3 sts = 1 inch; 4 rows = 1 inch in mock rib pattern

Stitch pattern:

Mock rib stitch:

(Multiple of 2 sts)

Row 1: (RS) K1, p1.

Row 2: (WS) P.

Stockinette for collar: K all sts every rnd.

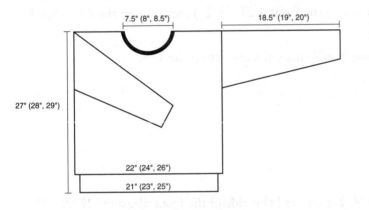

This schematic shows the pieces you'll need for the Boyfriend's Sweater.

> **JAZZING IT UP**
>
> The instructions for the smallest size appear outside the parentheses. Directions for the other two sizes are in respective order inside the parentheses. Be sure to follow the directions for the size you're making.

Back:

With size 10.5 ndl, CO 67 (73, 79) sts.

Row 1: (K1, p1), k1.

Row 2: P.

Work these 2 rows for a total of 8 rows.

Change to size 11 ndl, and continue working st patt until piece measures 27 (28, 29) inches or desired length. Do not BO. Place all sts on a st holder or spare ndl. Set aside.

Front:

Work same as back until piece measures 24 (25, 26) inches and rep Row 2.

Shape neckline:

Work 39 (43, 46) sts, and place last 11 (13, 13) sts on a st holder. You'll pick up these sts for the collar.

Work in st patt across remaining 28 (30, 33) sts. Work each shoulder separately.

P back.

On next 3 RS rows, BO at the neck edge as follows:

> 3 sts 1×
>
> 2 sts 1×
>
> 1 st 1×

Remember to stay in the st patt, as some RS rows may not begin with a k st. 22 (24, 27) sts remain. Work in st patt until this side of the front is 27 (28, 29) inches from the CO edge. Put these sts on a st holder.

Rejoin yarn to other side. This time, you'll shape the neck from the WS.

On next 3 WS rows, BO:

> 3 sts 1×
>
> 2 sts 1×
>
> 1 st 1×

Work in st patt on remaining 22 (24, 27) sts until this side of the front measures 27 (28, 29) inches from the CO edge. Ready sts to do a three-ndl bind-off.

Three-needle bind-off for shoulder seams:

Place sts from front and back on separate size 11 ndls. Place them so RSs are facing each other.

Three-ndl bind-off 22 (24, 27) sts from the shoulders, continue, and BO 23 (25, 25) sts from the back, and three-ndl bind-off the rem 22 (24, 27) sts from the other shoulder. FO.

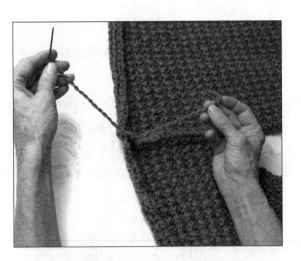

After finishing the three-needle bind-off, tie a knot with the loose ends. You weave them in later.

The three-needle bind-off creates beautiful, even shoulder seams.

Sleeves:

Sleeve length 18½ (19, 20) inches.

This is a good time to check the sleeve length. Put the unfinished sweater on the boyfriend, and measure from the edge of the knitted shoulder down to the wrist to confirm the necessary sleeve length. If you need to lengthen the sleeves, add rows before starting sleeve shaping. Once you confirm the correct sleeve length, you are ready to pick up the stitches.

Measure down 11 (11½, 12½) inches from shoulder seam. With size 11 ndl, pick up and k67 (69, 75).

P back. Work 2 rows in st patt.

Begin sleeve shaping:

On next RS row, work as follows: k1, ssk, work in st patt to last 3 sts, k2tog, k1.

JAZZING IT UP

Remember to stay in the stitch pattern as you're making the sleeve decreases. Watch for the pattern as you begin each RS row.

Work this decrease row every 4th row 16× (17×, 18×) total, until 35 (35, 39) sts rem.

Purl back after last dec row. Change to size 10.5 ndls, and work in st patt for 8 (6, 8) rows, working dec row 1 (0, 1) more time, until 33 (35, 37) sts rem.

BO. If desired, leave a length of yarn about twice the total length of the sleeve and side of the sweater you can use to sew up this seam.

Rep for the other sleeve.

When finished, the sleeve is a perfect extension from the shoulder.

This is what the wrong side should look like.

Collar:

The collar is intentionally designed to curl, giving it a soft edge.

With size 11 circular ndl, and starting at top of left shoulder with RS facing, pick up and k14 sts down to the holder, k11 (13, 13) sts from the holder, and pick up and k another 14 sts up to the right shoulder. Pick up and k23 (25, 25) sts across the back (62 [66, 66] sts).

PM and begin k in the round in stockinette for 6 rnds. Change to size 10.5 circular ndls, and cont k in the round for another 4 rnds. BO evenly and not too tightly.

Finishing:

Using the whipstitch, sew the sleeve seams first and then the side seams. Be sure the WS is facing you.

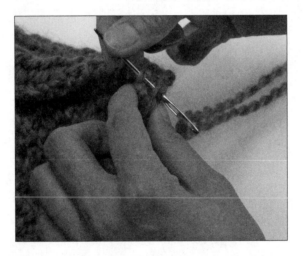

Weave in the ends. Lightly block the seams.

Blocking is a technique used to straighten uneven seams, stretch your knitted fabric to a specific size so you can sew it to another piece, or correct the shape of a section or whole garment. The three methods of blocking include wet blocking, steam blocking, and spray blocking. Each has a specific use.

This sweater should come together easily without needing much blocking. To finish it up, set a steam iron on the wool setting, place a towel over the section to be blocked, and go over the seams very lightly with the iron. It shouldn't need very much. Be careful not to get it too wet. The idea is to relax the fibers just a little so the seams are perfect.

The Least You Need to Know

- Measure the person the garment is for before starting your project. These measurements are essential to a good-fitting garment.
- Measure again, just to be sure!
- Be sure your gauge is accurate for the yarn and needles you're using.
- Monitor your stitch pattern throughout the process of knitting your sweater so the stitches all match up properly.

The Anatomy of a Jacket

In This Chapter

- Knitting garments
- Making horizontal buttonholes
- Finishing touches: a simple crocheted edge

This chapter leads you through the process of making a garment out of several pieces. Now that you've come this far, it should be a comfortable next step. You'll add the horizontal buttonhole to your repertoire along with the finishing touch of a crocheted edge. These are skills that you'll undoubtedly use many times in future projects. Your command of the craft grows stronger with each step in the process.

A Five-Piece Puzzle

The first project many new knitters begin with is a scarf. It's a simple rectangle, and most beginner knitters can create a lovely scarf by learning just one stitch pattern.

In spite of what some may say, moving on to a garment, like a jacket, isn't really a big leap. Think of it as simply making larger shapes and attaching them together. If you can make a scarf, you can make a jacket. It's just a five-piece puzzle: one back, two fronts, and two sleeves. Adding buttonholes is as simple as binding off a few stitches in one row and picking them up again in the next row.

New knitters are often afraid of making garments, but really, they shouldn't be. My good friends Cindi and Jerry, who own Yarn and Fiber in Derry, New Hampshire, insist that customers jump into making garments right away. "When we register students for beginning knitting classes, we don't allow them to start with boring scarves or blankets. We want them to work on something they will enjoy every day. Knitting is supposed to be creative and fun. We have them pick out yarns they really like as well as a pattern that appeals to them. There is tremendous pride in finishing a garment. People think they are not capable of making anything but a scarf, but they're wrong, and they find that out."

Making Buttonholes

If you're making a jacket, you'll also need to make buttonholes to hold the jacket closed. There are several ways of making buttonholes, but the two-row horizontal method is very common and quite easy.

Swatch It!

With worsted weight yarn and size U.S. 10 or 10.5 needles, CO 20 sts.

K 2 rows.

Begin stockinette for 6 rows. K the 1st 2 and last 2 sts on all p (WS) rows for selvedge edge.

With RS facing you, k3, BO 4 (the last k st will pass over the next k st), k to end.

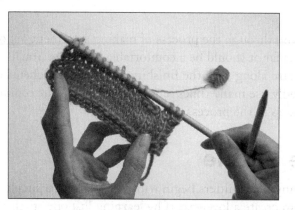

(WS) K2, p to BO sts, CO 4 sts, k2.

K the next row and then BO.

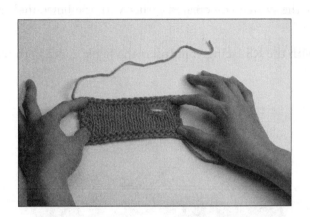

There. An easy buttonhole!

Assembling a Garment

Once you have all the pieces of your garment knitted, it's time to assemble them:

1. Attach the back and front pieces at the shoulder, either with three-needle bind-off, kitchener stitch, or whipstitch.

2. Attach the sleeves.

3. Sew on the button opposite the buttonhole.

4. Add any finishing touches, edging, pockets, etc.

5. Weave in all loose ends.

> **UNRAVELING**
>
> Be careful when assembling a garment that you pay close attention to the right side, wrong side, and the direction of each section. It's very easy to mix these up and put a sleeve wrong side out or a panel upside down.

Single Crochet (sc) Edging

The addition of crochet stitches can enhance your knitting and give it a lovely finishing touch. In addition to being decorative, a single crochet (sc) edging can help smooth out uneven or curled edges, too.

Swatch It!

For this swatch, use the swatch you created earlier with the buttonhole and a size H crochet hook.

Begin at a corner with the RS facing you. Insert the hook under both parts of the st, and pull up a loop.

Insert the hook into the next st, draw up a new loop, and pull it through the 1st loop. You should have 1 loop on the hook. Make the loops loose, and do not pull them tight.

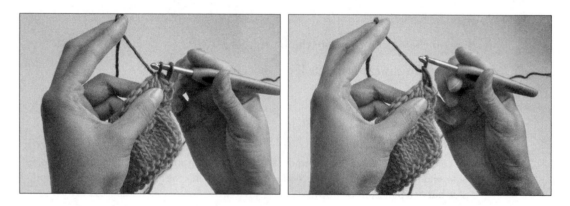

Rep step 2 all around the swatch.

When you arrive at a corner, ch2 and insert the hook into the next st on the upcoming side.

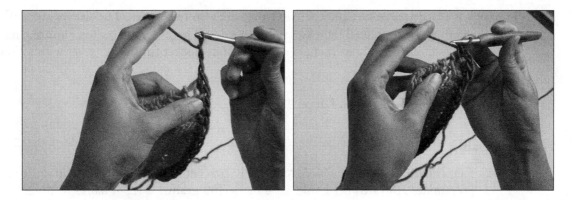

Cut the yarn, pull the tail through the last loop, and weave in the end.

 A STITCH IN TIME

In 2007, the Museum of Arts and Design in New York mounted an exhibit titled *Radical Lace and Subversive Knitting*. The exhibit featured a wide range of works created by fiber artists from seven countries. They published a book with photographs of the show that's very inspiring. More recently, the Hunterdon Art Museum in New Jersey mounted a show titled *Knitted, Knotted, Netted.* It featured the innovative work of artists on the forward edge of textile and fiber arts. Museums often select work by fiber artists for their exhibitions, and these pieces can serve as inspiration for all of us who love to knit.

Project: On-the-Town Jacket

This lightweight three-season jacket is knit using the purl ridges stitch pattern throughout the piece.

This jacket is a wonderful accessory for pants or skirts and is just the right weight for summer through fall.

The back is a large rectangle, and the two fronts are also rectangles. The sleeves are worked from the cuff up, with gradual increases on both sides. There is large button closure, and the collar edges fold over. A single crochet edge and single pocket finish the jacket with a flourish.

Finished size:

Small: 38 (Medium: 44, Large: 48) inches

Materials:

5 (5, 7) hanks Aslan Trends, Artesanal; 40 percent cotton, 30 percent alpaca, 30 percent polyamide; 218 yards per hank; 3.5 ounces (100 grams); 2 (2, 3) hanks Midnight Black, Color 19; 2 (2, 3) hanks Stone Grey, Color 71; 1 (1, 1) hank Candy Apple Red, Color 3528

U.S. 10 (6mm) circular and straight needles

Additional needle needed for three-needle bind-off

U.S. I (5.5mm) crochet hook

Large black button about 2 inches in diameter or length

3 stitch holders

Long straight pins

Large-eye darning needle

Gauge:

4 sts = 1 inch

Stitch pattern:

Purl ridges:

Row 1: (RS) K.

Rows 2 and 4: P.

Row 3: K1, *p1, k1; rep from * to end.

Abbreviations:

beg	beginning
ch	chain
inc	increase
sc	single crochet

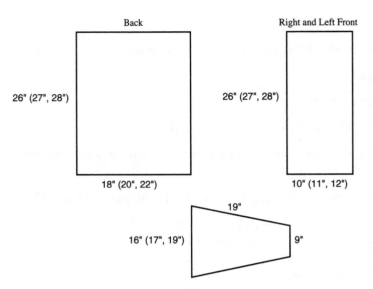

With this schematic for reference, the pieces to the puzzle are quite easy to manage.

Back:

CO 80 (88, 96) sts in Midnight Black, Color 19.

Work purl ridges pattern for entire back until piece measures 26 (27, 28) inches.

Do not BO. Place all sts on st holder.

Right front:

CO 44 (52, 56) sts in Midnight Black, Color 19, and work purl ridges st patt until piece measures 17 inches. End after p row.

Buttonhole row 1: K4, BO4, finish row in patt.

Buttonhole row 2: P to BO sts, CO 4, p to end.

Resume st pat, and cont until piece measures 26 (27, 28) inches.

Do not BO. Place all sts on st holder.

Left front:

CO 44 (52, 56) sts in Midnight Black, Color 19, and work purl ridges st patt until piece measures 26 (27, 28) inches.

Do not BO. Place all sts on st holder.

JAZZING IT UP

I usually knit both fronts and, later, both sleeves on the same circular needle. This helps me ensure they're both the same length. If you choose to do this, just be sure the yarn for each doesn't get tangled in the process. Put each ball into a separate container, and watch for twisting when you turn your work.

Sleeves (make 2):

CO 40 (44, 48) in Candy Apple Red, Color 3528, and work k1, p1 rib for 6 inches.

Inc row: K1, m1 *k6, m1 (6 times); k5, m1, k1.

Change to Stone Grey, Color 71, and p back.

Begin purl ridges st patt in next row. Maintain the st patt as you add sts.

Inc 1 at the beg and end of the 4th (purl) row of the pattern. Cont with this inc until you have 66 (74, 82) sts.

Inc 1 at beg and end of the 8th row (p row) until piece measures 18 (19, 20) inches from CO.

BO evenly.

Pocket:

The pocket is the same number of sts for all sizes.

CO 40 sts using Candy Apple Red, Color 3528.

Work purl ridges st patt 8 times.

Work 6 rows of garter st (k all rows), and BO.

Assembly:

1. Transfer sts of back to circ ndl.

2. Transfer sts of right side to ndl.

3. Align the two pieces so the WS are on the outside (RS facing each other) and the ndls are pointing in the same direction. Be sure the buttonhole edge is at the middle of the garment.

4. Commence three-ndl bind-off from the shoulder edge. BO 26 (30, 34) sts. The remainder of the sts on the front are for the fold-over collar.

5. Rep for left front. Begin at the shoulder, and BO 26 (30, 34) sts. Continue BO through the neck.

6. Lay out the piece flat with WS up. You may need to lightly steam the pieces so they lay flat.

7. Pin a sleeve in place, making sure the middle of the sleeve is in line with the shoulder seam.

8. Sew the sleeve to the side of the garment. Rep for other sleeve.

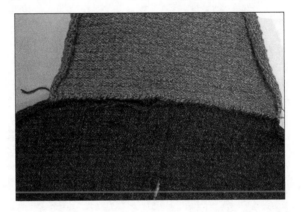

9. With WS out, sew up sleeve from cuff to underarm. Rep for 2nd sleeve.

10. Working from the underarm down, sew up side seams. Leave a 4-inch side opening at the bottom of each side.

11. Turn the garment right side out, and attach the button on the opposite front side of the buttonhole.

12. Using Candy Apple Red, Color 3528, and the crochet hook, begin the sc edge in the flap between the back section and the right front. (Beginning here makes it easy to hide the loose ends later.) Work the sc edge around the entire piece. When you arrive at a corner, ch2 and return to sc.

13. Sew the pocket on whichever front panel you prefer.

14. Weave in all loose ends.

The Least You Need to Know

- Most knitted garments are simple puzzles with just a few pieces to assemble.
- Horizontal buttonholes involve binding off a few stitches in one row and picking them up on the next row.
- A crocheted edging can add a special touch to your garment.
- Always check your gauge!

Advanced Techniques

In Part 5, we look at intarsia, entrelac, and felting. These techniques are fun, exciting, and much easier to learn than you might think.

The intarsia chapter explores knitting details with color. Think paintings of landscapes, flowers, street scenes, or abstract images. All these can be created using your yarn and needles with intarsia techniques. Earlier we learned about changing yarns for striping. Now you can change yarns to create images and designs.

Knitted geometric designs are created using a technique called entrelac. You can use a yarn that's dyed many colors or change yarn colors for different shapes. You'll impress yourself, along with everyone else, with a simple entrelac scarf.

Learning about felting takes your knitting in a new direction. Felting enables you to create strong, three-dimensional pieces like bags and bowls. To felt your work, you combine hot, soapy water with agitation. The results are a little unpredictable and always exciting.

Chapter 19

In This Chapter

- Beyond color—intarsia!
- Working with color keys and graphs
- Using bobbins
- Twisting yarns to avoid holes and problems

Incorporating color and design into your work can greatly enrich your knitting. Many fabulous books and patterns show off designs ranging from objects to natural environments to abstract images. You can go well beyond stripes and blocks of color into very complex and challenging knitted masterpieces.

In this chapter, we work with intarsia, a technique for working with multiple colors in one section of knitting. The key to successful intarsia work is winding the yarn so the knitting of one color moves seamlessly without interruption to the next color from the right side view.

Getting Started with Intarsia

With intarsia, you can create colorful designs in your work with many different yarns. Usually knitted in stockinette stitch, the yarns are kept to the back of your work, and by twisting the yarns at each color change, you prevent holes from appearing in your knitted fabric.

By keeping the yarn wound on bobbins, the yarns don't get tangled, and you can work with smaller lengths of yarn rather than a full skein.

Color keys are very helpful. A chart printed in color contains a key showing the shading and name or number for each color. If the chart is in black and white, the colors in the key are noted by symbols. If you decide to use different colors than those specified in the pattern, you should make your own color key. Most pattern charts are small, so using a ruler or straight edge can help you keep your place. Post-it notes are handy for place-keeping, too. And they don't move if you bump the pattern!

Different colors of yarn are wound on bobbins in small amounts to be used row by row.

Colorwork patterns are usually designed on graph paper. Each square or space in the paper represents a stitch, and each line represents a row. Right side or odd-numbered rows begin on the right; wrong side or even-numbered rows begin on the left.

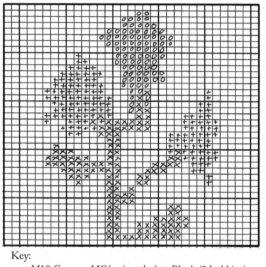

This color chart and key indicates the colors for each row.

Key:
M10 Creme - MC(main color) = Blank (3 bobbins)
M69 Old Sage - Color A, symbol = ✕ (3 bobbins)
M102 Orchid Thistle - Color B, symbol = ✛ (2 bobbins)
M105 Pink - Color C, symbol = ○ (1 bobbin)

Swatch It!

Let's start with a small piece to get used to working with bobbins. You'll need U.S. 10.5 straight needles, 3 bobbins, and 2 contrasting yarns. Use the darkest yarn for the background and main working yarn. In the instructions, I refer to this as the main color (MC) and the contrasting yarn as A. This keeps things simple while you learn the technique for twisting the yarn.

Let's start with a vertical line pattern:

1. Wind about 2 yards of MC yarn (the background yarn) on 2 bobbins. Wind 2 yards of yarn A (the contrasting yarn) on a bobbin.

2. With MC, CO 20 sts and k 4 rows (garter stitch edge) and 2 rows of stockinette.

First color change row (RS—knit):

3. With RS facing you, k6 with MC.

4. Change colors by dropping MC and picking up A from under MC.

5. K6 with A. Drop A and pick up 2nd bobbin of MC from under A.

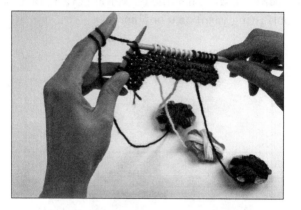

6. K6.

7. When you turn your work, be sure the bobbins don't tangle. Arrange them in order of knitting.

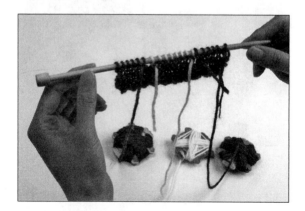

Color change on WS:

8. P6 with MC.

9. Change to A by dropping MC and picking up A from under MC.

10. P6 with A; change back to MC, and p6.

Repeat these 2 rows two more times to complete the block pattern. You have now learned how to change colors using the bobbins in a vertical line pattern. Cut yarn A, leaving a 4-inch tail.

Now let's work a color with a diagonal shape. Continue on the same swatch with the stockinette stitch for 4 rows with MC. This will put a little distance between the first color changes and this next part. You'll use MC and A yarns again.

Diagonal line patterns:

1. With RS facing you, k9; change to color A by dropping MC and picking up A from under MC; k2 with A; change to MC, picking it up from under A, and k9.

2. Now you'll begin the diagonal on the WS. When you're on the purl side, bring the new color over the *top* of the old for a left diagonal and *under* the old color for a right diagonal: (WS) p8; change to A, bringing it over MC, p4; change to MC, picking it up from under A, and p8.

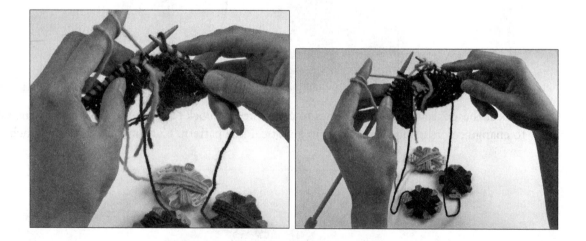

3. Working on the knit side (RS), you bring the new color *over* the old on the right diagonal and bring the new color *under* the old on the left diagonal: (RS) k7; change to A.

4. K6 with A; change to MC, and k7.

5. (WS) P6; change to A and p8; change to MC and p6.

You should now be able to see a triangle forming on the RS of your work.

When you've finished a section, cut the yarn from the bobbins, leaving 4-inch tails. Wind them into the corresponding color at the back, making sure this additional yarn doesn't show in the front. If you're working with very small sections, wind in what you can and cut the tail shorter. Just be sure your stitches are secure.

Project: Bobble Pillow with Intarsia Appliqué

This Bobble Pillow has an intarsia section that you sew on during the assembly. The intarsia pattern is quite simple and gives you some practice with bobbins. If you want to try your hand at a different pattern, find some graph paper and work out your own design!

If the pattern suits you, feel free to change the colors to match your living room or bedroom. The Brown Sheep Company has a rainbow for you to choose from.

This pillow is knit in two pieces. The back of the pillow is knit in bramble stitch, and the front is knit with a bramble stitch border and a 6×6-inch stockinette center.

The intarsia appliqué is knit separately, set into the stockinette center, and stitched down. An I-cord is knitted and stitched as a frame around the appliqué.

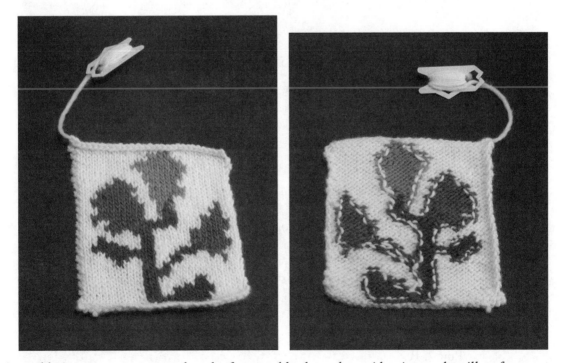

Assembly is easy: you sew together the front and back on three sides, insert the pillow form, and sew up the last side.

Finished size:

16×16 inches (with pillow form inside)

Materials:

1 skein Brown Sheep Company, Lanaloft; 100 percent wool; 160 yards per skein; 7 ounces (198 grams); Color LL-87, Catamaran Seas (for pillow)

Brown Sheep Lamb's Pride Worsted; 85 percent wool, 15 percent Mohair; 109 yards per skein; 4 ounces (113 grams); 1 skein each: Color M-10, Crème (MC); Color M-69, Old Sage (A); Color M-102, Orchid Thistle (B); Color M-105, RPM Pink (C) (for intarsia insert)

1 pair U.S. 10.5 needles

1 pair U.S. 7 needles

2 stitch markers

6 bobbins

14×14-inch pillow form

Gauge:

Pillow in bramble stitch using 10.5 needle and Lanaloft: 4 sts = 1 inch; 4 rows = 1 inch

Intarsia insert in stockinette using U.S. 7 needle and Lamb's Pride Worsted: 4.7 sts = 1 inch; 6 rows = 1 inch

Stitch pattern:

Bramble stitch:

Row 1: P.

Row 2: K, p, k into next st, p3tog.

Row 3: P.

Row 4: P3tog, k, p, k into next st.

Stockinette:

Row 1: K.

Row 2: P.

Pillow back:

With size 10.5 ndls and Lanaloft, CO 58 sts.

Keeping 1st and last st in stockinette, work center 56 sts in bramble stitch.

Work 14 reps of bramble stitch or until piece measures 14 inches, and BO firmly.

Pillow front:

With size 10.5 needles and Lanaloft, CO 58 sts.

Work as for back for 4 reps.

Work next row as follows: k1, bramble st 16 sts, PM, k24, PM, bramble st 16 sts, k1.

Work next row as follows: p1, bramble st 16 sts, SM, p24, SM, bramble st 16 sts, p1.

Continue in this manner, working the edge sts and center 24 sts in stockinette and 16 sts on each side in bramble st, for 6 reps.

Return to working the edge sts in stockinette and center 56 sts in bramble st for 4 reps. BO firmly, leaving a length of yarn a little over 2 yards long you can use to sew the pillow front and back together. Set aside.

Intarsia insert to measure 6×6 inches:

Wind bobbins:

> 3 Crème (MC): 3 or 4 yards each
>
> 3 Old Sage (A): 2 yards each
>
> 2 Orchid Thistle (B): 2 yards each
>
> 1 RPM Pink (C): 2 yards

With size 7 ndl and Crème, CO 28 sts.

Begin following color graph, starting on Row 1, k from right to left, each square representing 1 st. Use a separate bobbin for each color section. Be sure to cross yarns in the intarsia knitting method to avoid holes when changing colors. Work graph through Row 42.

BO, leaving 1 yard Crème for attaching intarsia insert to pillow front.

Weave in all ends. Lightly steam piece so it lays flat and measures 6×6 inches.

Make an I-cord using Lanaloft long enough to make a frame around the insert (approximately 24 inches). BO.

Assembly and finishing:

If necessary, block stockinette inset of pillow front to measure same as intarsia insert. To do this, pin border of stockinette inset to ironing board or towel to desired measurements, and steam. Let piece dry before removing pins.

Sew intarsia insert onto pillow front.

Sew I-cord around border of intarsia insert, following the line where the insert and pillow front meet.

Pin pillow front and back together over pillow form. Sew in place.

The Least You Need to Know

- Intarsia is a knitting technique for incorporating color in your work with the use of bobbins.
- The key to great intarsia work is the way you cross the yarns when changing from one color to the next.
- Color charts and keys indicate which color to use for each stitch in a row, so pay close attention!

Entrelac

In This Chapter

- The wonders of entrelac
- Understanding short rows
- Making shapes and connecting them

For you math enthusiasts, this chapter should be great fun. Entrelac is a knitting technique wherein you knit geometric shapes in different directions. If math isn't your strong suit, don't worry. The patterns have a certain logic to them and are easy to follow.

The results can be stunningly beautiful, especially for garments that are completely knitted in entrelac. In this chapter, you learn to make a simple scarf, but you can easily enlarge it for a shawl.

What Is Entrelac?

Finding the origin of the word *entrelac* took some sleuthing. Many sources say it's French, but *entrelac* does not appear in any English or French dictionary. I contacted my friend Frédérique Crestin-Billet, owner of Maison Sajou in Versailles, France, and author of many books on the needle arts.

She wrote, "Despite its French name, the entrelacs knitting comes from Scandinavia, in particular from Finland. The technique was used to knit bonnets, mittens, or tall socks. The entrelacs can be confused with lace, but it's a completely different technique." She also told me that there should be an "s" on the end of the word and that it's a compound word: *entre* means "between," and *lacs* is a French word from the eleventh century meaning "a kind of cord or string used to bind parchments and make netting to catch animals."

Today, we know it as a knitting technique that uses short rows to create interlocking triangles and rectangles. The resulting patterns look woven, almost like basket-weaving. If you use a variegated yarn or change colors for different blocks, the final piece can be a brilliant burst of color.

Entrelac may look daunting, but it's really nothing more than knitting a series of small shapes in a specific sequence. Once you understand how to make each shape and the sequence of shapes, the rest is easy. You begin with the bottom row of base triangles, work the next row of triangles and rectangles, and so on.

Swatch It!

To begin this swatch, you need worsted weight yarn and size 8 or 9 straight needles. You can use the same yarn throughout or change colors for different sections.

The sample swatch and practice project include base triangles, left-side triangles, right-slanting rectangles, right-side triangles, left-slanting rectangles, and top triangles.

Here are a few things to remember:

- When you see *sl 1*, you are to slip 1 knitwise on the RS and purlwise on the WS.

- Several of the shapes begin with a slip stitch for a selvedge edge. This makes it easier to pick up stitches from that section.

- In all the previous patterns, you've been turning your work at the completion of a row, putting the right needle with all the stitches into your left hand. When you see *turn* in this pattern, you may only be 1 or 2 stitches into the row. Turn your work anyway. This creates the necessary short rows for making that shape.

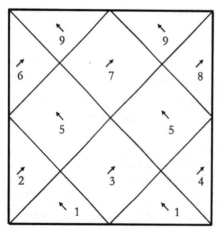

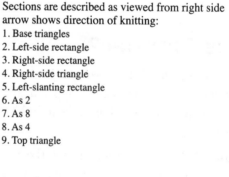

Sections are described as viewed from right side arrow shows direction of knitting:
1. Base triangles
2. Left-side rectangle
3. Right-side rectangle
4. Right-side triangle
5. Left-slanting rectangle
6. As 2
7. As 8
8. As 4
9. Top triangle

This diagram indicates the direction and the sequence of the shapes you knit.

CO 14 sts.

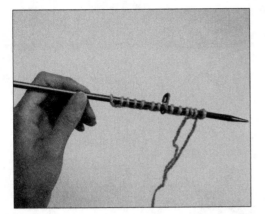

When you begin, place a stitch marker after the seventh cast-on stitch. This is where the division between the two base triangles will be.

Base triangles:

These are worked from the RS. Make 2.

Row 1: K1, turn.

Rows 2, 4, 6, 8, 10, and 12: These are WS rows. Pull sts.

Row 3: Sl 1, k1, turn.

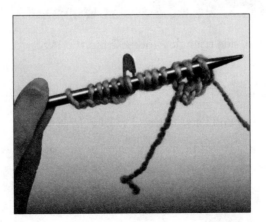

Row 5: Sl 1, k2, turn.

Row 7: Sl 1, k3, turn.

Row 9: Sl 1, k4, turn.

Row 11: Sl 1, k5, turn.

Row 13: Sl 1, k6. *Do not turn your work.*

You've just completed the first base triangle. With the next 7 stitches on the left needle, make the other base triangle using the same pattern.

Next you will make a left-side triangle, worked from the WS.

Left-side triangle:

Row 1: (WS) P1, turn.

Row 2: (RS) K1 f&b (front and back), turn (2 sts).

Row 3: P1, p2tog, turn. (You will be purling together one of the new sts you just made along with 1 st from the base triangle.)

Row 4: K1, m1, k1, turn.

Row 5: P2, p2tog, turn.

Rows 6, 8, 10, and 12: K to last st, m1, k1.

Row 7: P3, p2tog, turn.

Row 9: P4, p2tog, turn.

Row 11: P5, p2tog, turn.

Row 13: P6, p2tog. *Do not turn your work.*

Next, you'll make right-slanting rectangles. In this piece, you'll need to pick up stitches. A good trick to use for picking up stitches in entrelac is to use the left needle to lift up the 2 strands of the selvedge stitch from front to back. You can then insert the right needle into the opening and purl the stitch.

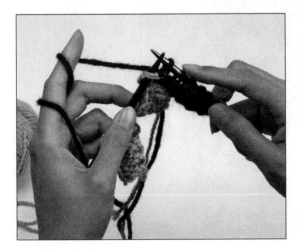

It's helpful to use the left needle to open the stitch for the right needle to work the purl stitch.

Right-slanting rectangle worked from the WS:

Row 1: Pick up and purl 7 sts along the edge of the base triangle.

Row 2 and all RS rows: K7, turn.

Row 3 and all WS rows: Sl 1, p5, p2tog. (Each time you p2tog, 1 st will include a picked-up edge and the other sts from the base triangle.)

Continue working Rows 2 and 3 until you've used all the sts by p2tog. *Do not turn your work* when this is completed.

Right-side triangle worked on the WS:

Row 1: (WS) Pick up and p7 along the edge of the base triangle.

Row 2 and all RS rows: K all sts, turn. Row 2 will be k7, turn. The number of sts will decrease by 1 on every RS row.

Row 3: Sl 1, p4, p2tog, turn.

Row 5: Sl 1, p3, p2tog, turn.

Row 7: Sl 1, p2, p2tog, turn.

Row 9: Sl 1, p1, p2tog, turn.

Row 11: Sl 1, p2tog, turn.

Row 13: P2tog, turn, and transfer this st to the right ndl. (It serves as the 1st st in the next section.)

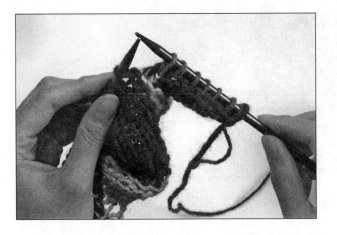

The stitches on the right needle are holding the newly formed right-side triangle.

Left-slanting rectangles worked on the RS (make 2):

Row 1: (RS) Pick up and k7 along selvedge edge of next section. You're beginning with a st from the right-side triangle, so you only need to pick up 6 more sts.

Row 2 and all WS rows: P7, turn.

Row 3 and all RS rows: Sk1, k5, ssk, turn. Your 1st sl st is from the picked up section and the 2nd is from the next section. Just as a reminder, ssk means you slip, slip, and then knit the 2 sl sts tog.

Repeat Rows 2 and 3 until all sts have been combined by the ssk in each row. *Do not turn your work* after the last ssk.

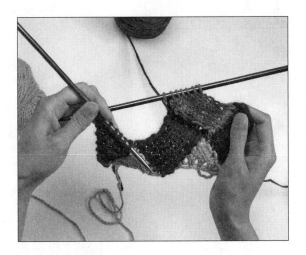

For the second left-slanting rectangle, repeat the instructions from Row 1, picking up 7 sts along the selvedge edge of the next rectangle.

For the remainder of the swatch, repeat the shapes in the following order:

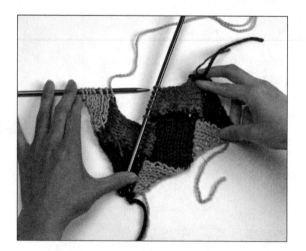

Left-side triangle.

Right-slanting rectangle.

Right-side triangle.

Top triangles:

The top triangles are worked on the RS. Make 2.

Row 1: Pick up and k6 along selvedge edge of next triangle, and turn (total of 7 sts).

Row 2 and all WS rows: P all sts, turn.

Row 3: K2tog, k4, ssk, turn.

Row 5: K2tog, k3, ssk, turn.

Row 7: K2tog, k2, ssk, turn.

Row 9: K2tog, k1, ssk, turn.

Row 11: K2tog, ssk, turn.

Row 13: Sl 1, ssk, pass the 1st sl st over the ssk (*psso*) leaving 1 st on the right ndl. *Do not turn your work.* Use the remaining st as the 1st st of next top triangle. After you complete the last triangle, FO.

The abbreviation **psso** indicates passing the slipped stitch over other stitches.

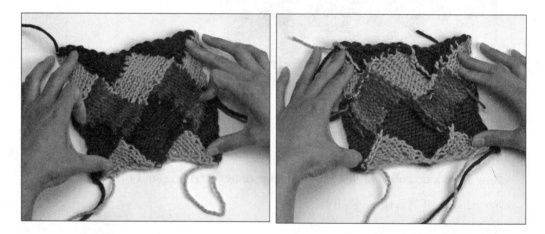

Project: Entrelac Scarf

Now that you've made your entrelac swatch, this scarf should be quite easy. And it's sure to have *wow* factor whenever you wear it.

The yarn you use makes the color changes for you. If you want to make a longer scarf, just add another skein.

Finished size:

>8 inches W×57 inches L

Materials:

>3 skeins Noro, Silk Garden; 45 percent silk, 45 percent kid mohair, 10 percent lamb's wool; 110 yards per skein; 1.6 ounces (50 grams)
>
>U.S. 9 (5.5mm) straight needles

Gauge:

>Not critical

CO 21 sts.

Work in the entrelac pattern, following the directions for each shape in the swatch.

The sequence is as follows:

3 base triangles

*1 left-side triangle

2 right-slanting rectangles

1 right-side triangle

3 left-slanting rectangles

Rep from * until scarf is near desired length.

Work 3 top triangles to finish the scarf. Remember that the top triangles must be made after completing a right-side triangle.

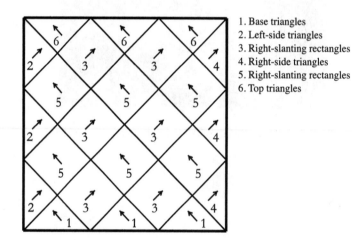

1. Base triangles
2. Left-side triangles
3. Right-slanting rectangles
4. Right-side triangles
5. Right-slanting rectangles
6. Top triangles

The Least You Need to Know

- Entrelac is a technique involving knitting geometric shapes in a sequence.
- With entrelac, you don't have to change yarns with each shape unless you're changing colors. You connect one shape to the next by binding off and picking up stitches.
- Entrelac can be used for all kinds of projects, from scarves to blankets to garments.

Felting Your Knitting

In This Chapter

- The felting process
- Choosing fibers and yarn for felting
- The importance of improvising and experimenting
- Adding embellishments—the garden variety

If you've owned any wool sweaters, you know you need to take special care of them, hand-washing or dry-cleaning them only if you want them to last. Invariably though, a sweater will end up on the wrong pile and be thrown in the wash with other clothes. The result is a shrunken, somewhat stiff, formerly loved garment that can never be worn again. That old friend of a sweater went through a felting process.

Intentionally putting a knitted wool piece through that same process can produce some spectacular results. Knitting for wet felting is not an exact science because so many variables are involved. Different yarns, water hardness, detergent, and washing machines all contribute to the outcome. Fortunately, with many projects it won't matter, and you can roll the dice and have a great time with this technique.

How Felting Works

Felt is an amazing cloth. It can be soft and pliable or tough and sturdy. It is the oldest form of fabric known to man, with documented remnants dating back 6,500 years. People have used felt for everything from clothing to shelter. Nomads in central Asia still use it for their yurts, tentlike structures that shelter them from the often severe environment.

Felting is also an amazing process. Felt begins most commonly with sheep wool, although other animal fibers can be used. Just like human hair, the wool fibers are covered with scales. When these scales are exposed to heat and moisture, they become soft. If you add a little agitation, the scales on a strand of fiber can lock onto other strands in close proximity. Once locked together, they are joined permanently. Felting, or combining wool, hot water, a little soap, and some agitation, can be accomplished by hand or in the washing machine.

The most exciting aspect of the felting process is that it's somewhat unpredictable. Each time you try it, the results will be different—sometimes slightly different and other times drastically different. Variables include the machine you use, variances in the water temperature, the length of time you have the piece in hot water, the kind of soap you use, and, of course, the yarn. If you use two different yarns in a project, they may felt at different stages.

The Best Fibers to Use for Felting

Wool is your best-bet yarn material for felting. Alpaca, llama, silk, and other animal fibers also felt, but with varying levels of success. For the best results, begin with wool.

When buying wool yarn for felting, be sure it's 90 to 100 percent wool. If it's a blend, try to buy a blend that includes wool and another animal fiber. Do not purchase superwash wool, because this yarn is treated in such a way that it intentionally will not felt.

Avoid bleached white wool as well. The bleaching affects the scales, or cuticle, and prevents successful felting. Some colors will felt faster than others. Making test swatches of the yarn you want to use will help you determine how well the yarn will felt and what will happen to the color and texture.

> **A STITCH IN TIME**
>
> Cottons and acrylics don't felt, but they can be used as textural or colorful accents in a piece.

Testing the Fiber

Creating swatches gives you a general idea of how a specific yarn behaves during the felting process. It's not an exact science, however.

Begin by knitting two swatches on needles two sizes larger than the yarn label indicates for a normal knitting gauge. You want to make the swatches about 10×10 inches. Put one of the swatches in your washing machine in a mesh lingerie bag. (Using the mesh bag cuts down on the amount of fiber that will invade the workings of your machine.) Along with the mesh bag, put a couple of old towels, a tennis shoe, and a very mild detergent in the machine. Let it run on a full hot/cold cycle.

When it's finished, take a good look at your swatch. Did your swatch shrink more vertically than horizontally? Did the color change? Are the stitches still noticeable, or did they felt together so well that they can no longer be seen?

Repeat the process with the second swatch. This time increase or decrease the amount of time in the wash. Is there a difference?

Let's look at two examples. In each pair, the same yarn was used for both swatches, which started out the same size.

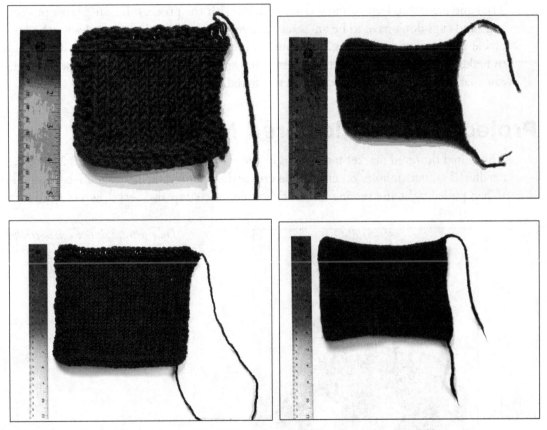

The left swatches are knitted but not felted. The right swatches are knitted and then felted.

As you can see, the felted swatch shrunk more from top to bottom than side to side. This is not unusual. In general, your felted piece will shrink overall about a third of the size of the original swatch.

> **A STITCH IN TIME**
>
> Knitting bloggers tell some interesting stories about their experiences. One such blogger, Kathy (runswithneedles.wordpress.com), says she enjoyed the knitting for her soon-to-be-felted bag but things went very wrong. The bag shrunk so much in height that at the end of the felting process, it looked like a bra. "I don't know about you," she writes, "but I don't wish to carry a bag that looks like a bra …." She continues to write about the lessons she learned during the process and finishes with a great solution to her problem: "I will salvage what I can from this monstrosity. I plan to get out the scissors and cut the bag up into place mats (for animal dishes) and coasters (for me, obviously)."

Trial and error will lead you to a comfort level with the process. Because most projects like bags and rugs don't have to be an exact size, you'll most likely be pleased with the results. If you tackle a more complex project like slippers where exact dimensions really matter, you will need to make detailed notes about the variables and spend time becoming as knowledgeable of your raw materials as you can. Once the yarn is felted, there's no turning back!

Project: Felted Flowered Market Tote

This felted flowered market tote is knit in the round on U.S. size 13 (9mm) 24-inch circular needles. Two buttonholes on either side create the opening for the felted I-cord shoulder strap. When pulled tight and resting on your shoulder, the strap also serves as a closure for the bag.

Once felted, this tote will be strong enough to hold just about anything you need to carry, including groceries or a laptop.

I felted the body of the bag and the shoulder strap in the washing machine and the flower embellishments by hand in the kitchen sink. Because this is knit on large needles and the felting process is quick, this is a great evening or weekend project.

Finished size:

17 inches W×12.5 inches H×3.25 inches D

Materials:

Brown Sheep Company, Shepherd's Shades; 100 percent wool; 131 yards per skein; 3.5 ounces (100 grams): 2 skeins SS281, Eggplant (Color A); 2 skeins Ss283, Boysenberry (Color B)

Brown Sheep Company, Lamb's Pride Worsted Weight; 85 percent wool, 15 percent mohair; 190 yards per skein; 4 ounces (113 grams): 1 skein M10, Crème (Color C); 1 skein M102, Thistle (Color D); 1 skein M105, Pink (Color E); 1 skein M69, Old Sage (Color F)

JAZZING IT UP

If you have worsted weight wool in colors that complement the body of the bag, use them. You can also incorporate novelty yarns in the flowers.

U.S. 13 (9mm) 24-inch circular needles

U.S. 10.5 (6.5mm) straight needles

U.S. 10.5 (6.5mm) double-pointed needles

U.S. N crochet hook

Large-eye darning needle

Rubber gloves

Gauge:

Not critical

Stitch pattern:

Garter stitch: K all rows.

Stockinette stitch: K 1 row, p 1 row.

Body of bag:

Begin with the bottom gusset. With A, CO 50 sts and k 20 rows in garter stitch.

Pick up sts around the edge of the gusset as follows: 10 sts along each short edge and 50 sts along the long edge (120 sts).

Begin knitting in the round with stockinette stitch. PM at beg of rnd.

Cont with A for 4 rnds.

Change to B for 4 rnds.

Change to A for 4 rnds.

Change to B for 10 inches.

Change to A for 2 rnds.

Buttonhole round—2 buttonholes on each side:

Marker should be at the beginning of the rnd, ready to k one of the long sides. K20, BO5, k20, BO5, k30; BO5, k20, BO5, k10.

K20, CO5, k20, CO5, k20, CO5, k20, CO5, k10.

K next rnd.

Change to B for 5 rnds.

Decrease row:

*K2, k2tog; rep to end of rnd (90 sts).

Combine colors A and B for 2 rnds.

BO, alternating between knitwise and purlwise.

I-cord shoulder strap:

With A on dpn, CO 5 sts, leaving a 7-inch tail.

*K 1 row, p 1 row; rep from * until piece measures 60 inches.

BO, leaving a 7-inch tail.

Time to felt!

Insert the body of the bag and the shoulder strap into a mesh lingerie bag, and place in the washing machine with a couple of old towels, and an athletic shoe. Wash in a mild detergent (no bleach) for a complete "normal" cycle with hot wash and cold rinse. When the cycle is complete, check the pieces and be sure they've felted enough. The fabric should be thick and the stitches obscured.

Do not put them in the dryer. Instead, stretch them into the desired shape and let them air dry.

This is the body of the tote before felting.

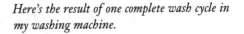

Here's the result of one complete wash cycle in my washing machine.

When the pieces are all dry, thread the I-cord strap through the buttonholes. Tie the ends together securely with the tails. With the darning needle, thread the tails into the inside of the I-cord.

Felted flowers, stems, and bow:

The felted flowers are three sizes of the same pattern. The stems and bow are made of I-cords.

Adding felted flowers to the front of the bag in different sizes and colors creates more visual interest.

Small flower:

With E, CO 20 sts on 10.5 straight ndls.

Rnd 1: K all sts.

Rnd 2: *K1 f&b; rep to end (40 sts).

Rnd 3: Rep Rnd 2 (80 sts).

BO loosely, leaving a 7-inch tail.

Medium flower:

With C, CO 30 sts.

Rnd 1: K all sts.

Rnd 2: *K1 f&b; rep to end (60 sts).

Rnd 3: Rep Rnd 2 (120 sts).

BO loosely, leaving a 7-inch tail.

Large flower:

With D, CO 45 sts.

Rnd 1: K all sts.

Rnd 2: *K1 f&b; rep to end (90 sts).

Rnd 3: Rep Rnd 2 (180 sts).

BO loosely, leaving a 7-inch tail.

Assembling the flowers:

Twist the knitted piece into a swirl shape.

Using the darning needle, sew the swirl in place.

Rep for each flower.

Stems and ribbon: I-cords:

CO 3 sts on dpn, and create I-cord stems for each flower and a bow to tie them together. Each cord should be approximately 8 inches long.

Felting the flowers, stems, and bow:

Place a large bowl in the sink and fill it with very hot water. Put on a pair of rubber gloves to protect your hands during this process. Add some mild dish detergent to the hot water. I use Ivory Dishwashing Soap for this project. Put the flowers, stems, and bow cord into the hot water, and agitate the water with your gloved hands. Be patient; this may take a little while.

If the water cools, pour off some of it and refresh with hot water. If the felting isn't going fast enough, rinse with cold water and repeat the process.

When the pieces are felted, rinse them again in cold water. To be sure that all the soap is out, you can add a little vinegar to the cold water. This will neutralize any soap left in the pieces.

When everything is dry, sew the pieces onto the body of the bag with strong thread. I used linen thread.

That's it! You should have a stunning little number to take to the market.

The Least You Need to Know

- Felt is formed when the wool is heated and agitated, allowing the scales on a strand of fiber to interlock with the strands around them.
- Felting has been used to create strong cloth for thousands of years.
- Wool is the best fiber to knit for felting.
- When you felt your knitted piece, you'll find it shrinks to about a third of the size of your original piece.

Yarns and Tools

Everything you need to know about yarn, needles, and other fun tools is covered in Part 6.

Here we learn the basics about fiber and yarn so when you go to your local yarn shop, you'll have a good idea of what you're getting. There's so much great yarn out there available in so many places, it can be a little confusing and overwhelming.

The great thing about knitting is that you can begin with just a ball of yarn and a pair of needles—a pretty small investment. After you progress and really begin knitting with abandon, you will need some additional needles, tools, and accessories. You don't have to acquire all these at once. Buy them as you need them. I give you a guide for what you need when, with descriptions of the tools and their uses.

Everybody makes mistakes. No matter how long you have been knitting, dropped stitches, wrong stitches, unintentional things happen. In the last chapter, I show you how to correct common problems you might encounter in your knitting.

Fun with Fiber

In This Chapter

- A guide to yarn weights
- Fiber basics: natural and synthetic
- Novelty yarns and handspun
- Shopping for fiber

My friends, family, and co-workers know of my yarn addiction. They're seldom surprised when they see me carting in yet another bag of yarn. I'm especially distracted by beaded yarn; or yarn that has metallic threads gleaming through strands of wool; or great big luscious hanks of wool, silk, or alpaca. Hand-dyed fibers are especially alluring, and the vendors who paint their hanks are really creating works of art. In fact, I once had a woman buy a hand-dyed hank of yarn just to hang on her wall!

Hand-spinners are also a wonderful group. They're known to incorporate bits and pieces of miscellaneous fibers into a hank of wool. I once bought a hand-spun skein that included shredded dollar bills!

Once you begin exploring fibers, you'll quickly discover that the choices are infinite!

All About Yarn Weights

The Craft Yarn Council of America (CYCA) is a group made of publishers and fiber, needle, and hook manufacturers who worked together to "set up a series of guidelines and symbols to bring uniformity to yarn, needle and hook labeling." Their goal: to make it easier for the industry to provide consistent information to consumers. One of their accomplishments has been to set up categories of yarn by weight, gauge ranges, and recommended needle and hook sizes. That information, presented in the following table, is quite helpful.

Standard Yarn Weight System

Yarn Weight Symbol and Category Name	0 LACE	1 SUPER FINE	2 FINE	3 LIGHT	4 MEDIUM	5 BULKY	6 SUPER BULKY
Type of yarns in category	Fingering, 10-count crochet thread	Sock, fingering, baby	Sport, baby	DK, light worsted	Worsted, afghan, aran	Chunky, craft, rug	Bulky, roving
Knit gauge* range in stockinette to 4 inches	33 to 40** sts	27 to 32 sts	23 to 26 sts	21 to 24 sts	16 to 20 sts	12 to 15 sts	6 to 11 sts
Recommended needle (metric)	1.5 to 2.25 mm	2.25 to 3.25 mm	3.25 to 3.75 mm	3.75 to 4.5 mm	4.5 to 5.5 mm	5.5 to 8 mm	8 mm and larger
Recommended needle (U.S.)	000 to 1	1 to 3	3 to 5	5 to 7	7 to 9	9 to 11	11 and larger
Crochet gauge* ranges in single crochet to 4 inches	32 to 42 double crochets**	21 to 32 sts	16 to 20 sts	12 to 17 sts	11 to 14 sts	8 to 11 sts	5 to 9 sts
Recommended hook (metric)	Steel*** 1.6 to 1.4 mm	2.25 to 3.5 mm	3.5 to 4.5 mm	4.5 to 5.5 mm	5.5 to 6.5 mm	6.5 to 9 mm	9 mm and larger
Recommended hook (U.S.)	Steel*** 6, 7, 8 hook B to 1	B to 1 E to 4	E to 4 to 7	7 to I to 9	I to 9 to K to 10½	K to 10½ to M to 13	M to 13 and larger

* Guidelines only. This reflects the most commonly used gauges and needle or book sizes for specific yarn categories.

** Lace-weight yarns are usually knitted or crocheted on larger needles and books to create lacy, openwork patterns. Accordingly, a gauge range is difficult to determine. Always follow the gauge stated in your pattern.

*** Steel crochet books are sized differently from regular books—the bigger the number, the smaller the book, which is the reverse of regular book sizing.

Not all yarn manufacturers are using this labeling system, though. European and South American yarns include some of the information such as yardage, weight of the ball or skein, and suggested gauge and needle size. The word *suggested* is the key here, regardless of where the yarn comes from.

As I mentioned in Chapter 12, gauge is personal, and you must check how the yarn works for you on the needles.

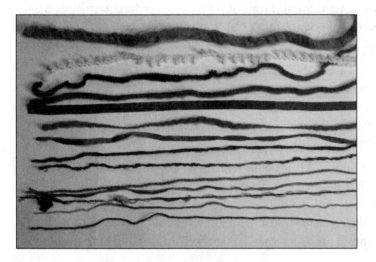

Just like different needle sizes affect your gauge, so do various weights and thicknesses of yarn.

JAZZING IT UP

A great resource for all of your yarn questions is Yarndex. According to yarndex.com, it's the "ultimate yarn resource" with information and profiles of more than 5,000 yarns. At the site you can review information about the manufacturer, fiber content, weight, yardage, and all the colors available for every fiber.

A Closer Look at Natural Fibers

Natural fibers are divided into two categories:

- Animal (protein)
- Vegetable (cellulose)

Let's examine each in a little more detail.

Animal Fibers

You're probably familiar with some, if not all, of the most popular animal fibers:

- Wool
- Alpaca

- Mohair

- Cashmere

- Angora

- Silk

The yarns these fibers produce can be used for all kinds of projects, including garments, handbags, scarves, shawls, blankets, and just about anything else you can think of.

The most common of the animal fibers is wool. Wool is so ubiquitous that in some regions of the world all yarn is called wool, regardless of the actual fiber. Wool fibers come from sheep, and there are many varieties of these fiber-producing animals. Some wool fleeces are coarse, while others are very soft and fine. Wool yarn is available in all weights and, because it takes dyes well, in myriad colors. Wool blends are also quite popular. Manufacturers combine the wool fibers with other natural or man-made fibers.

Alpacas are members of the camelid family. Alpaca cousins llamas, camels, and vicunas also produce fiber for yarn, but alpaca fiber has become the popular choice from this group. Alpacas are commonly found in South America, and the bulk of alpaca yarn is imported from there. There is a growing community of alpaca farms in the United States, and more and more breeders are processing their fiber at domestic mills for the U.S. market. Alpaca fiber is extremely soft, warm, and insulating.

A STITCH IN TIME

The first alpacas were imported into the United States in the 1980s. Now alpaca breeders are in about every state, and some states have hundreds of breeders. Northern Ohio is home to the largest number of alpaca farms and the greatest number of alpacas. No wonder it's known as "Little Peru."

Mohair is a warm, lightweight fiber that originates from the fleece of the angora goat. These goats were originally from Turkey. Texas is now a big producer of angora goats and the largest producer of mohair.

Cashmere is the luxurious fiber combed from the bellies of the cashmere goat. These goats inhabit the mountains of China and Tibet. The yarn made from these fibers is deliciously soft and warm. It's often combined with other fibers, especially wool.

Angora rabbits provide fluffy fiber for beautiful yarn. Like the process for gathering the fiber from cashmere goats, the rabbits are combed, not shorn like sheep. Angora is usually combined with other fibers for easier spinning. Angora fiber is relatively expensive.

Silk has a protein structure, like other animal fibers. Silk worms spin fine threads and form an all-encompassing cocoon. After all that work, the worm is killed and the cocoon is unwound.

Its filaments are spun into beautiful yarns and ribbons that are divinely smooth and intensely colorful. Silk fibers are often combined with wool and other fibers.

Fiber from yaks, Alaskan musk oxen (spun for quiviut), mink, beaver, buffalo, and chinchilla also has been worked into yarn. You can learn more about these wild fibers through *Wild Fibers Magazine* at wildfibersmagazine.com.

Vegetable Fibers

Now for the most popular vegetable fibers:

- Cotton
- Linen
- Bamboo
- Raffia

Each has its own characteristics.

Cotton yarns are light and absorbent but less flexible and stretchy than wool. It's best used for lightweight sweaters or tops. Sometimes manufacturers mix cotton with synthetics to increase elasticity, making it easier to work on the needles. Knitters look to cotton and cotton/synthetic blends for baby clothes and anything made for people allergic to wool.

Linen is stiff but softens up as you wear it. It does well in the washing machine, and the more it's used, the better it feels. I have a knitted linen skirt I adore, and it gets better and better with age, never losing its color or shape.

In the past few years, bamboo yarns have entered the market with great success. The yarn is very soft and easy to knit. Colors tend to be more muted, but the yarns are lovely and reasonably priced.

Raffia is a type of straw and is available in bright colors. It is quite stiff and used primarily for handbags and embellishments.

Working with Man-Made Fibers

Nylon, polyamide, polyester, rayon, acrylic, and metallics—these are a few of the man-made fibers you can knit with. Sometimes they're blended with natural fibers, or with each other, and other times they're 100 percent of the yarn. These fibers are strong and can mimic natural fibers in look and feel.

One of my favorites is rayon. When dyed, rayon takes the color magnificently, and the knitted fabric is brilliant and stunning.

Interesting Alternatives: Wire, Cloth, and Plastic

Experimenting with different materials can lead you to very interesting discoveries. For example, you can knit necklaces with thin silver wire and knit rag rugs with torn cloth. A friend of mine is experimenting with knitting rope for a hammock. Many patterns are available online for knitting totes out of plastic shopping bags. You can also find patterns for knitting items like tote bags from old VCR tape!

If you come up with an interesting idea for knitting recycled materials, groups on Ravelry.com would love to hear from you. Some of the larger groups are Raveler's Recycled Knits and Crochets, Alternative Yarns, and Unravelers. All of them share ideas and patterns, so there's a wealth of information here.

JAZZING IT UP

You can find many free patterns online for totes you can knit using plastic shopping bags. The results are quite impressive, and you can feel good about your recycling efforts!

Playing with Novelty Yarns

Here's where yarns get really interesting. You can give your knitting punch, bling, or textural interest simply by using novelty yarns. These yarns may have beads, little flags, ornaments, or paillettes worked into them. Sometimes the base is wool or silk.

Yarns that feature embellishments knotted right on the thin string are known as carry-along yarns. You knit them along with another thicker yarn to add texture, color, or both. These yarns can make a project unique, and what fun you can have!

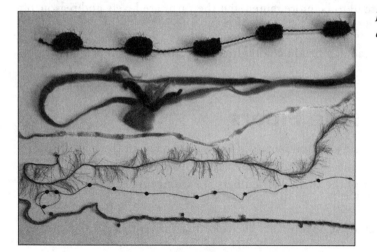

Here are some of my favorite novelties. You can see the range of possibilities here.

As a new knitter, my 12-year-old niece was fascinated with a yarn that had great big poufs on it. Her motivation to knit was inspired by this yarn. She quickly picked up the basic skills on plain yarn and moved in on the challenge of working with the pouf yarn. Some novelty yarns are more difficult to knit with than others, and this one wasn't easy. She ripped out her work a few times before conquering the yarn, but it was worth it. In the end, she gave the completed pouf scarf to a friend and made another for herself.

Manufactured Versus Hand-Spun Yarns

Many domestic and foreign companies are supplying yarns to the U.S. market, each with a range of fibers and colors in its collection. You can depend on these larger manufacturers to provide quality and consistency with their products. When you're knitting a large project, try to buy all the yarn you need when you begin, making sure the *dye lot* is the same for all the balls or hanks so they all match perfectly. If you run short, the company can sometimes match the dye lot, or you might find another store with the same lot number.

> **DEFINITION**
>
> When yarn is dyed, the manufacturer or artist dyes a certain amount at a time, making a record of the batch and giving it a number called a **dye lot.** Each dye lot may have color variations from other dye lots, so if you can, buy all your yarn from the same dye lot for a project.

If you can't find the dye lot in stores, you can post your need on Ravelry. Maybe another knitter has some of the same yarn he or she is willing to share (or sell). If all else fails and the dye lot you can get is a color that's very different from the original, *improvise!* Here are some ideas for alternatives you can consider if you run out of yarn for sleeves:

- Consider making both sleeves shorter than the pattern indicates.

- Change the color of the sleeves to a contrasting color.

- Add a different color for the cuffs, and use the original color for the other part of the sleeve—or vice versa.

- Can the sweater idea! You just knitted a gorgeous vest!

Those are some ideas for sleeves, but think about what you can do for other pieces. I once ran out of yarn before finishing the trim on a cashmere shawl. I had some lovely beaded yarn that blended well with the original color, so I cut up what I had of the remaining color for the fringe and added lots of the beaded yarn. The fringe became a glittering complement to the finished piece.

There's also a recent groundswell of hand-spinners who are supplying hanks of yarn to local shops and also selling their wares online. Many are selling their yarns on Etsy.com and through knitting and crochet communities like Ravelry.com. I've also purchased hanks from spinners at fiber shows. These yarns are tremendously varied and are a real treat to knit. If you want to use them for a whole project, be sure you order everything you need at once. If you run short, getting additional hanks that match what you have may be impossible.

One of my favorite hand-spinners lives in Milwaukee, and I met her at a fiber show. She had this hank of yarn spun with shredded dollar bills, and I just had to have it!

Shopping for Fiber

In addition to the outlets I mentioned earlier (Etsy.com, Ravelry.com, etc.), you also can purchase yarn in hobby and craft stores, some larger department stores, fiber shows, and of course, online.

Your local yarn shop (LYS) is the best place to begin, though. Go in and feel the fibers. Match smooth yarns with novelties. Venture into new color combinations and experience new textures. The owners or employees there will likely love to help you find just what you're looking for.

After all, if you buy yarns you like, the knitting will come easy.

The Least You Need to Know

- Working with the Craft Yarn Council of America, companies are in the process of standardizing yarn labeling. The label tells you the weight of the yarn, needles you need, and the fiber content, along with other information.
- Fibers are divided into three main categories: animal fibers, vegetable fibers, and manmade fibers. Some yarns are a combination of all three.
- You can knit with nontraditional materials like rope, metal, and plastic. What else can you think of?
- Be careful of dye lots. If you're making a garment, buy a little more yarn than you think you need, just to be sure it all matches. This mostly applies to solid-color yarns.

Your Knitting Kit

In This Chapter

- All about needles
- Measuring tools you'll need
- Rounding out your tool collection

Any successful craftsperson has a tool box or kit. Knitters are no exception. But what tools do you need in your knitting kit, especially if you're just starting out knitting?

Some tools you must have in your kit. Others might come in handy but are far from *necessary* if you don't want to splurge right now. You can certainly pick up the basics and take your time acquiring the special items you might want later.

A good example of this is a yarn swift. Do you really need it? Maybe not. But is it helpful? You bet it is!

The Needles You Need

Like most people, I started knitting and picked up the necessary tools as I needed them. You don't have to start with a complete set of straight, double-pointed, and circular needles in all sizes to begin experiencing the craft. A few basics will serve you well in the beginning.

Needles are available in wood, metal, plastic, and bamboo. Before investing in a complete set, try out different materials to see what works best for you. Sometimes metal needles will be too slippery for some yarns, while other yarns will stick on wooden needles.

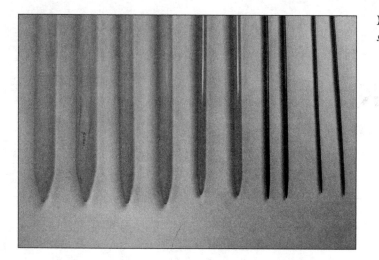

You can find needles in all sorts of different sizes and materials.

Specialized needles, with very sharp points, are available for lace knitting. Square needles are available, too, and many people feel they are easier to work with. Clearly, you have many options. Your local yarn shop (LYS) will have many needles available for you to try.

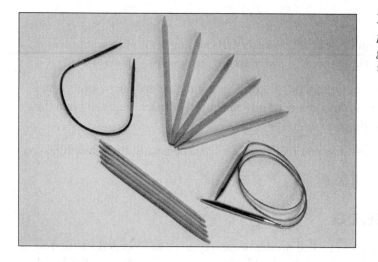

You'll probably add circular and double-pointed needles to your collection after you've gotten the hang of working with straight needles.

If you pick up a European pattern, it may not have the U.S. needle size equivalent listed. What do you do? Simply convert the European metric sizes to U.S. sizes, as shown in the following table.

U.S. Needle Size	Metric Needle Size
0	2mm
1	2.25mm
2	2.75mm
3	3.25mm

U.S. Needle Size	Metric Needle Size
4	3.5mm
5	3.75mm
6	4mm
7	4.5mm
8	5mm
9	5.5mm
10	6mm
11	8mm
13	9mm
15	10mm
17	12mm
19	15mm
35	19mm
50	25mm

On straight metal needles, the size is usually found on the end knob. Wooden, bamboo, and circular needles are stamped with the sizes, and after you use them for a while, the size markings tend to wear off. For this reason, it's good to have a needle gauge for confirming the size of your needles.

This needle gauge is handy when you need to identify the size of your needles.

Helpful Tools to Have on Hand

In addition to needles and a needle gauge, other tools are helpful with your projects. You don't need the fancy versions of these tools. Functionality is the most important characteristic.

Measuring Tools

Measuring tools are essential from the beginning. Be sure you buy a tape measure that has inches on one side and centimeters on the other.

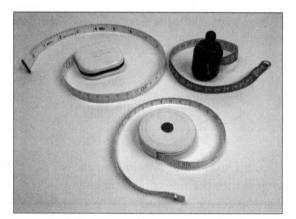

Stitch Markers

Stitch markers range from the simple to the decorative. Be careful of the size, though. Not all of them will fit all sizes of needles. Be sure you purchase and use what you need for your project. If you're working on large needles and can't find markers that fit, make your own out of yarn or metal ties.

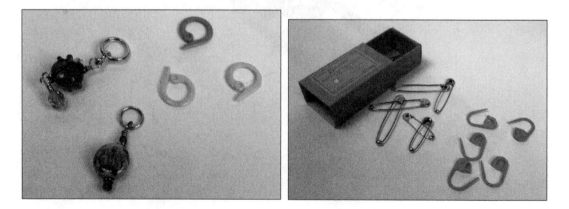

Safety pins are a great alternative to stitch markers.

Stitch Holders

Stitch holders, handy for … well … holding stitches, are available in plastic and metal and come in a variety of sizes.

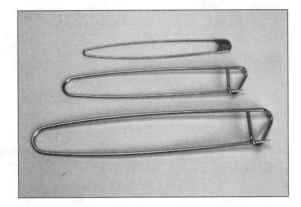

Large-Eye Darning Needles

Darning needles are necessary for finishing seams and weaving in ends. Some are straight while others have a curved end. See what works best for you.

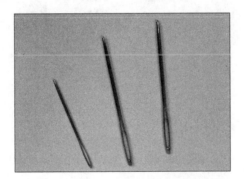

Pins

Straight pins come in handy when you're joining together sections of garments. Plastic pins are very kind to the yarn.

Scissors

Having a great pair of scissors is imperative. If you plan on traveling with them, the current rule for the airlines limits the blade to 4 inches. Check with your airline before bringing them to the airport.

Cable Needles

You probably won't need cable needles right away, but if you catch the cabling bug, these will come in very handy!

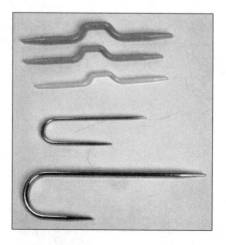

Point Protectors

Point protectors hold your stitches on your needles and are especially helpful when working with circular needles. Use them when you're ready to put down your knitting.

Crochet Hooks

Crochet hooks are great friends of knitters. Use them for adding embellished edges and for rescuing fallen stitches. Buy a few to begin with, including a small (C or D), a medium (I or J), and a large (N or O).

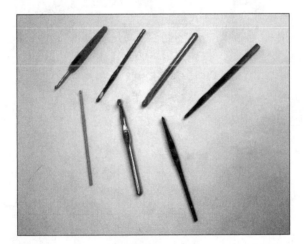

Stitch and Row Counters

Some knitters love their stitch and row counters. I prefer using a pencil and paper or marking right on my patterns.

Bobbins

If you like intarsia knitting or have leftover yarns you want to save, bobbins are the perfect tool. You can buy plain or decorative bobbins—or make them yourself!

Yarn Swift

Yarn swifts assist you in converting a hank of yarn into a ball. Most are adjustable to accommodate different hank diameters.

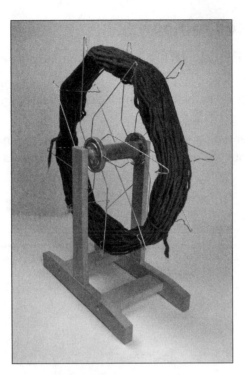

Organizer for Tools and Projects

You can find organizers and project bags to suit every taste and budget. You'll find lots to choose from at your LYS or local craft store.

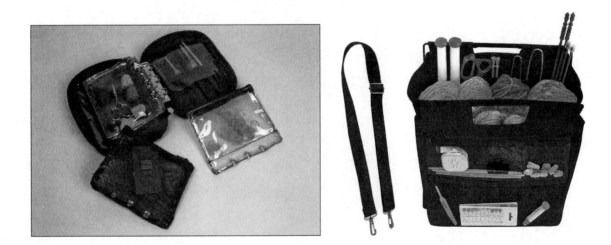

The Least You Need to Know

- The most important tools you need to begin knitting are needles. Try out the various kinds at your LYS.
- Other tools to pick up in the beginning include a measuring tape, scissors, and a large-eye darning needle.
- You can add other tools and accessories according to the material lists on your patterns—or your whim!—but you only need the basics to get started.

Correcting Common Problems

In This Chapter

- Mistakes happen, and you can fix many of them
- Correcting common problems: changing knits to purls and purls to knits, dropped stitches, and tight cast-ons and bind-offs
- When all else fails, frog it!

With each project you tackle, you'll learn more and more about the craft of knitting—and eventually find that certain problems creep up on you more than once or twice. These common mistakes often have simple fixes.

If you see a knit stitch that should be a purl, you can knit your way back to the problem. If that stitch is a few rows back, you can change it—without ripping out your knitting! Sometimes you won't see a dropped stitch until many rows past the problem. Not to worry—you can fix that as well. There are also solutions for tight cast-ons and bind-offs. Finally, if you do have to go back a number of rows, you can do it without ripping out the whole section. All these fixes are covered in this chapter.

Knitting Your Way Back to a Problem

If you've noticed a mistake in the row on your needles, or even the row below, you can work your way back to the mistake by undoing each stitch, whether it's a knit or a purl, increase or decrease.

Let's say you have a purl stitch 3 stitches back.

1. Insert your left ndl in the st below the st on the right ndl.

2. Bring the st up on the left ndl and at the same time, pull the working yarn, releasing the st above it.

3. Rep until you arrive at the purl stitch. Undo the p st, place it on the left ndl, and k it. Then, simply finish the row.

Changing Knits to Purls and Vice Versa

Okay, you're moving right along through a stitch pattern and—*oops!*—you knit when you should have purled. If this occurs in the row you're working on, just go back to the stitch, undoing the stitches before it, and correct your mistake. If the problem is a few rows back, don't fret. It happens to all of us. Your crochet hook comes to the rescue.

To practice the rescue, create a swatch with about 15 rows of knitting. It's best to have about 12 stitches on your needle and work in stockinette stitch. Intentionally purl a stitch in the 10th row.

1. Work to the vertical point above and even with the incorrect st.

2. Now drop the st easily, and with your crochet hook ready, let the st go down to the row where the problem is.

3. Grab the st with the crochet hook, and weave it back up through the fabric in the correct direction.

After you have the dropped stitch on your needle, continue with the stitch pattern. It should look like nothing ever happened!

Picking Up Stitches

Invariably, you're going to drop a stitch, no matter how careful you are. Sometimes you'll notice this right away and catch it within a row or two. Other times, you'll see it hiding several rows below where you're working.

Either way, relax. It is fixable.

Picking Up a Dropped Stitch Down a Row—Knitwise

Interruptions happen. The phone or doorbell rings, someone calls from another room, or the timer on your oven goes off. You put down your knitting only to come back to dropped stitches that have loosened back a row or two. Yuck!

But never fear. Here's how you pick them up again.

1. Insert your left ndl through the front of the dropped st so it won't travel any farther.

2. Insert the left ndl under the loose strand directly above the dropped st.

3. With the right ndl, pull the dropped st over the strand and tip of the ndl.

4. Now k the st on the left ndl, and cont on.

Picking Up a Dropped Stitch Down a Row—Purlwise

Sometimes dropped stitches are more obvious on the purl side in stockinette stitch. It just pops out at you, and you can see the horizontal line from each row very clearly.

1. Insert the left ndl into the purl st.

2. Insert the left ndl under the loose strand. It should now be to the right of the dropped st on the left ndl.

3. With the right ndl, lift the dropped st over the strand and the point of the ndl.

4. Pull the strand through the st.

5. Transfer the st back to the left ndl and p it.

Picking Up Dropped Stitches Several Rows Down

This is where a crochet hook really becomes your best friend. When you notice a dropped stitch several rows down, first things first, stick a crochet hook into the stitch. You want to be sure the stitch doesn't fall any farther.

1. Position your work so you're above and at the same vertical point as the dropped st on the *knit side* of your work. Pull the ndls apart very gently, exposing the horizontal lines from each of the rows missing the st.

2. Look at your work carefully, and assess how many rows the st has fallen. The sample shows 4 loose strands, representing 4 rows.

3. With the crochet hook inserted into the dropped st, hook the strand right above the st and pull it through.

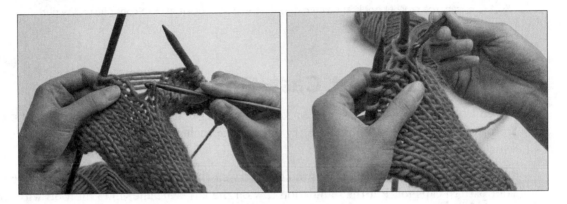

4. Pull next strand through, and rep until all the sts are picked up from the previous rows.

5. Repeat this process until you're at the same row as the ndls. Place the last st on the left ndl, and cont in the st patt.

JAZZING IT UP

Picking up stitches that have fallen several rows is easier on the knit side than on the purl side. To pick up purl stitches, simply turn your work to the knit side, pick up the stitches with the crochet hook, and when they're all in place, turn it back to continue on the purl side.

Dealing with Tight Cast-Ons

When I first started knitting, I cast on very tightly. This always made knitting the first row of a project very difficult. I think I was trying to make each stitch in the cast-on row the same, which only made me pay for it later.

If your foundation or cast-on row is too tight, try casting on with a needle one size larger than your pattern calls for. Put the foundation row on the larger needle, and knit it off with the needle specified in the pattern. No more tight cast-ons!

Dealing with Tight Bind-Offs

Tight bind-offs can be a serious problem. The bound-off edge might be a visible edge or an edge that needs to attach to another knitted piece in a sweater or jacket.

The solution? Same as with the tight cast-on, bind off with a needle one size larger than the one you're using for the body of the work.

The more practice you have binding off, the more you'll be able to control the tightness or tension of the working yarn and your stitches.

Frogging

When problems mount and seem unfixable or you just don't like the way your project is working out, you can get the greatest satisfaction by simply ripping out the stitches. This process is known as *frogging* because ripping out the stitches reminds them of the sound frogs make: *rip it, rip it, rip it!*

If you have to rip out a number of rows, you can still save the good part.

1. Weave a smaller ndl than you've been working with on your project into the right loop of each st in a row.

When you do this, be sure all the sts are in the same row and count to ensure you have all the sts in that row.

2. Pull out the working ndl, and unravel all the sts down to the small ndl.

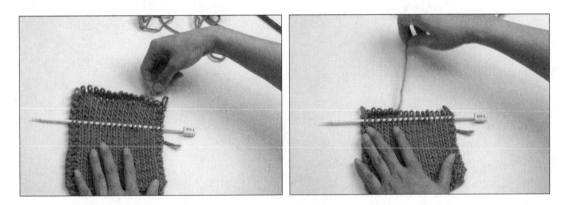

3. Pick up your work from this point and finish your project, frog-free!

Knitting should be a pleasurable activity. If you don't like the results, the yarn, or the pattern, don't fight with it. It's better to frog it and pass on the yarn to someone else. (I've given some yarns to charity and others to friends.) Go on to your next project and have fun.

You'll hear knitters moan about the UFOs in their closets. These are "unfinished objects" due to loss of interest, not enough yarn, or not enough time. In my workroom, I refer to them as WIPs, or "works in progress," and I always have several of them.

Once you get going with knitting, you'll find that some projects work up very quickly without much concentration, while others need your undivided attention. At the end of the day, I pick up a project I can knit while watching a mindless TV program. On a Saturday morning when the house is quiet, I pick up that jacket with the complex pattern of decreases.

Take pleasure in all of them. Hopefully the craft will become a satisfying and fulfilling part of your life, as it has mine.

The Least You Need to Know

- All is not lost! Many common mistakes can be very easily corrected.
- A crochet hook is your best friend when correcting many knitting mistakes.
- Picking up dropped stitches is easier on the knit side.
- When your knitting problems become unbearable, frogging is the best and most gratifying solution.

( ) Symbols used in a knitting pattern to indicate alternate measurements or instructions.

[ ] Symbols used in a knitting pattern to indicate you should work instructions within brackets as directed.

* Symbol used in a knitting pattern to indicate you should repeat instructions following the asterisk per directed.

2×2 rib A stitch pattern of 2 knit stitches followed by 2 purl stitches based on an even number of stitches. Rib patterns are commonly used for cuffs and collars of garments.

approx An abbreviation used in a knitting pattern to mean "approximately."

beg An abbreviation used in a knitting pattern to mean "begin" or "beginning."

bet An abbreviation used in a knitting pattern to mean "between."

bind off (BO) Closing the loops on your needle to form a finished edge.

BO An abbreviation used in a knitting pattern to mean "bind off."

bobbin A small cardboard or plastic piece for winding small amounts of yarn.

cast on (CO) The process of creating stitches in the foundation row.

cn An abbreviation used in a knitting pattern to mean "cable needle."

CO An abbreviation used in a knitting pattern to mean "cast on."

cont An abbreviation used in a knitting pattern to mean "continue."

Continental method A method of knitting that uses the left hand to guide and control the working yarn.

dec An abbreviation used in a knitting pattern to mean "decrease," "decreases," or "decreasing." To decrease, you reduce the number of stitches by knitting 2 or more stitches together.

dpn An abbreviation used in a knitting pattern to mean "double-pointed needle."

English method   The method of knitting that uses the right hand to hold and guide the working yarn.

entrelac   A knitting technique that involves stitching geometric shapes like rectangles and triangles.

foundation row   Creating the loops on the needle to begin the process of knitting.

frogging   Ripping out stitches. Think of the sound of *ribbit* (rip it).

garter stitch   A very common stitch pattern of knitting every row.

gauge   The number of stitches per inch and rows per inch.

I-cord   A knitted tube made on two double-pointed needles used for purse straps, edging, and embellishing.

in(s)   An abbreviation used in a knitting pattern to mean "inch(es)."

inc   An abbreviation used in a knitting pattern to mean "increase," "increases," or "increasing." To increase, you add stitches.

intarsia   A knitting technique that involves many color changes. The yarn is held at the back of the work on bobbins.

k   An abbreviation used in a knitting pattern to mean "knit."

k2tog   An abbreviation used in a knitting pattern to mean "knit 2 stitches together."

kf&b   An abbreviation used in a knitting pattern to mean "knit into front and back of stitch."

knitting or **purling stitches together**   A way of decreasing the number of stitches on your needle.

kwise   An abbreviation used in a knitting pattern to mean "knitwise"; requiring a knit stitch.

long-tail cast-on   A method of creating your foundation row.

m1   An abbreviation used in a knitting pattern to mean "make 1 stitch."

MC   An abbreviation used in a knitting pattern to mean "main color" of yarn.

p   An abbreviation used in a knitting pattern to mean "purl."

p2tog   An abbreviation used in a knitting pattern to mean "purl 2 stitches together."

pat(s)   An abbreviation used in a knitting pattern to mean "pattern(s)."

pf&b   An abbreviation used in a knitting pattern to mean "purl into front and back of stitch."

PM   An abbreviation used in a knitting pattern to mean "place marker" where a stitch marker should be inserted.

psso   An abbreviation used in a knitting pattern to mean "pass slipped stitch over."

pwise   An abbreviation used in a knitting pattern to mean "purlwise"; requiring a purl stitch.

rep An abbreviation used in a knitting pattern to mean "repeat(s)."

rnd(s) An abbreviation used in a knitting pattern to mean "round(s)."

roving Fiber that is combed but not spun.

RS An abbreviation used in a knitting pattern to mean "right side of work."

selvedge An edge created by adding a stitch or 2 at the beginning and end of each row of a stitch pattern, sometimes used as a decorative border, other times to aid in assembling a garment.

sk An abbreviation used in a knitting pattern to mean "skip."

sk2p An abbreviation used in a knitting pattern to mean "slip 1, knit 2 together, pass slipped stitch over the knit2 together (2 stitch decrease)."

skein Yarn wound in a circle and twisted into a loop.

skp An abbreviation used in a knitting pattern to mean "slip, knit, pass slipped stitch over knit stitch (1 stitch decrease)."

sl An abbreviation used in a knitting pattern to mean "slip." *See* slip (sl).

sl st(s) An abbreviation used in a knitting pattern to mean "slip stitch(es)."

sl1k An abbreviation used in a knitting pattern to mean "slip 1 stitch knitwise."

sl1p An abbreviation used in a knitting pattern to mean "slip 1 stitch purlwise."

slip (sl) An unworked stitch passed from the left needle to the right needle.

ssk An abbreviation used in a knitting pattern to mean "slip, slip, knit these 2 stitches together (1 stitch decrease)."

st(s) An abbreviation used in a knitting pattern to mean "stitch(es)."

stash A knitter's collection of yarn.

stitch pattern Combinations of stitches and rows that create visual textures and shapes in knitting.

stockinette stitch A stitch pattern of a row of knit stitches followed by a row of purl stitches.

tail The end of a knitted section that's been tied off.

tension The amount of pull or force you apply to each stitch.

tog An abbreviation used in a knitting pattern to mean "together."

top (or worsted top) Fiber that's combed and worked into a tube shape that can be knitted. It's not spun.

whipstitch An overhand sewing technique used for assembling pieces together.

working yarn The yarn coming from the ball or skein.

WS   An abbreviation used in a knitting pattern to mean "wrong side of work."

wyib   An abbreviation used in a knitting pattern to mean "with yarn in back."

wyif   An abbreviation used in a knitting pattern to mean "with yarn in front."

yarn weight   The thickness of the yarn.

yd(s)   An abbreviation used in a knitting pattern to mean "yard(s)."

yfwd   An abbreviation used in a knitting pattern to mean "yarn forward."

YO   An abbreviation used in a knitting pattern to mean "yarn-over."

Resources

Here are a few of my favorite resources. I'm sure you'll find many more to add to the list, but these are great places to begin.

General Shopping and Supplies

Your local yarn shop (LYS) is a treasure of materials and knowledgeable support for your projects. Visit yours often. Yarns are so tactile, and you'll enjoy the experience of getting to know different fibers at your LYS. Many of the stores have online shopping available as well. Two of my favorites are www.finepoints.com and www.yarnandfiber.com. When you travel, you can find local shops in *Fiber & Fabric Mania! A Travel Guide*, published annually by Direction Press. It includes some international locations as well.

Large craft retailers and hobby stores have the basics in yarn and supplies.

Many online stores offer big selections. My favorite is www.yarnmarket.com.

Yarn

My heartfelt thanks goes to the following yarn companies that have generously provided fiber for the projects in this book. I have worked closely with many of them over the years, and their support and encouragement is truly appreciated. I hope you enjoy working with their products as much as I have.

Aslan Trends
8 Maple Street
Port Washington, NY 11050
1-800-314-8202
www.aslantrends.com
(see Chapter 18's On-the-Town Jacket in
Artesanal)

The BagSmith
20600 Chagrin Boulevard, Suite 101
Shaker Heights, OH 44122
1-888-879-7224
www.bagsmith.com
(see Chapter 10's Little Black Bag or
Chapter 15's Cable and Rib Stole in Big
Stitch Alpaca Yarn)

Berroco, Inc.
14 Elmdale Road
PO Box 367
Uxbridge, MA 01569
508-278-2527
www.berroco.com
(see Chapter 17's Boyfriend's Sweater in
Peruvia Quick)

Brown Sheep Company, Inc.
100662 County Road 16
Mitchell, NE 69357
1-800-826-9136
www.brownsheep.com
(see Chapter 19's Bobble Pillow with
Intarsia Appliqué in Lanaloft and Chapter
21's Felted Flowered Market Tote in
Shepherd's Shades)

Coloratura Yarns
1006 Morgan Meadow Drive
Wentzville, MO 63385
1-866-765-9276
www.coloraturayarns.com
(see Chapter 11's Le Grand Beret in Merino
Flecks in Glitter Wiggles)

Fiesta Yarns
5401 San Diego Avenue NE
Albuquerque, NM 87113
505-892-5008
www.fiestayarns.com
(see Chapter 13's Diamond Lace Vest in
Flurry)

Trendsetter International
16845 Saticoy Street, Suite 101
Van Nuys, CA 91406
1-800-446-2425
www.trendsetteryarns.com
(see Chapter 12's My Favorite T and
Dropped-Stitch Shawl in Treasure)

Knitting Magazines

These magazines are filled with tutorials and patterns and inspirational ideas.

Interweave Knits
www.interweave.com

Knit 'N Style
www.allamericancrafts.com

Knitter's Magazine
www.knittinguniverse.com/knitters

Selvedge
www.selvedge.org

Vogue Knitting
www.vogueknitting.com

Knit-Related Websites

Many of these sites have patterns, blogs, video tutorials, and online knit-alongs. Others have extensive lists of national and international events. Ravelry is a worldwide online community of knitters and needle arts crafters.

The Daily Knitter
www.dailyknitter.com

Knitter's Review
www.knittersreview.com

Knitting Brain
www.knittingbrain.com

Knitting Daily
www.knittingdaily.com

Knitting Daily TV
www.knittingdailytv.com

Knitting Universe
www.knittinguniverse.com

Knitty
www.knitty.com

Men Who Knit
www.menwhoknit.com

Needle Travel
www.needletravel.com

Planet Purl
www.planetpurl.com

Ravelry
www.ravelry.com

Vogue Knitting
www.vogueknitting.com

Knitting Books

If you're starting a knitting library, these are good books to have on hand. Many knitting books are specialized on lace, socks, sweaters, afghans, and other projects. The books listed are great for beginning as well as advanced knitters.

Epstein, Nicky. *Nicky Epstein's Knitted Embellishments.* Loveland, CO: Interweave Press, Inc., 1999.

Melville, Sally. *The Knit Stitch.* Sioux Falls, SD: XRX Books, 2002.

Square, Vicki. *The Knitter's Companion.* Loveland, CO: Interweave Press, Inc., 1996.

Stitchionary Volume One, Knit and Purl. New York: Sixth & Spring Books, 2005.

Knit and Crochet Conferences

Once you catch the fiber bug, you'll be adding knit and maybe even crochet shows to your yearly calendar. These shows offer classes and workshops on a wide variety of topics and skills. You can try your needles on new techniques, or work on perfecting old ones. Each show has a marketplace with booths set up by local, regional, and national retailers.

The Knit and Crochet Shows are sponsored by the Crochet Guild of America and the Knitting Guild of America. The events have a wide range of classes to choose from and a good market-place, too. There are two shows, one on the East Coast and one on the West Coast. For more information, go to www.fiberartsmarket.com.

STITCHES shows are sponsored by XRX Publications. Four shows are held each year: STITCHES East, STITCHES West, STITCHES Midwest, and STITCHES South. Filled with classes and special events, these are well attended and lots of fun. You can find show times and classes at www.knittinguniverse.com.

Regional knit and crochet shows vary in size but not in enthusiasm. Watch in your local market. Sometimes shops will get together and sponsor a shop walk with coupons and treasure hunts taking you from one proprietor to the next. Prizes are given to those who visit all the shops on the list.

Fiber Festivals

Usually sponsored by state or local animal breeder associations, fiber festivals are great places to learn about natural fibers and the creatures that provide the raw materials. These are fascinating events. You can see shearing of animals at some of them, and many include weaving, spinning, crocheting, felting, and rug-making. Check with your state sheep, alpaca, or llama organizations for events near your home.

Maryland Sheep and Wool Festival is the mother of festivals. It takes place the first weekend in May and is the largest of all these events. Find out more at www.sheepandwool.org.

The New York State Sheep and Wool Festival is held in Rhinebeck, New York, during September and is another large event drawing people from all over the East Coast. Learn more at www.sheepandwool.com.

There are many other festivals throughout North America. You can find a comprehensive list of all of them at www.knittersreview.com.

Index

T–U–V

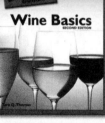

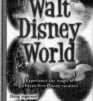